THE PSYCHOLOGY
OF ATTACHMENT

What do we actually mean by 'attachment'? How do different caregiving styles impact attachment in children? How do early caregiving experiences impact later development?

The Psychology of Attachment is an essential introduction to attachment, offering an accessible explanation of the theory, unpicking common misunderstandings, and providing a balanced overview of key research findings.

Topics covered include the following:

- The development of attachment during the first few years of life.
- The impact of different caregiving behaviours on children's attachment relationships.
- The influence of attachment relationships on children's behaviour and development.
- The development of attachment relationships from infancy to adulthood.
- Attachment in romantic relationships and religion.
- Attachment-based interventions.

This unique book introduces the reader to new ways of thinking about the role of relationships, caregiving, and child development, and the way in which they shape our lives.

Robbie Duschinsky is Associate Professor in the Department of Public Health and Primary Care, University of Cambridge.

He has conducted research in health and social care, history, and developmental psychology.

Tommie Forslund is a Postdoctoral Researcher in the Department of Psychology, Stockholm University. He received the Excellence in Attachment Research (EAR) dissertation award from the Society in Emotion and Attachment Studies (SEAS).

Pehr Granqvist is Professor of Psychology, Stockholm University. He has more than 20 years experience conducting and communicating attachment research. He has worked closely with leading researchers in the field of attachment. He received the 2023 William James Award from the American Psychological Association.

Cover image: © Getty Images

First published 2024
by Routledge
4 Park Square, Milton Park, Abingdon, Oxon OX14 4RN

and by Routledge
605 Third Avenue, New York, NY 10158

Routledge is an imprint of the Taylor & Francis Group, an informa business

© 2024 Robbie Duschinsky, Tommie Forslund and Pehr Granqvist

The right of Robbie Duschinsky, Tommie Forslund and Pehr
Granqvist to be identified as authors of this work has been asserted
in accordance with sections 77 and 78 of the Copyright, Designs
and Patents Act 1988.

British Library Cataloguing-in-Publication Data
A catalogue record for this book is available from the British Library

ISBN: 978-0-367-89654-6 (hbk)
ISBN: 978-0-367-89656-0 (pbk)
ISBN: 978-1-003-02034-9 (ebk)

DOI: 10.4324/9781003020349

Typeset in Bembo
by Apex CoVantage, LLC

For Erik Hesse, in friendship and respect

CONTENTS

INTRODUCTION

In *The Psychology of Attachment*, we aim to present an up-to-date summary of key conclusions from attachment theory and associated research. Ideas about attachment have become hugely popular across multiple academic disciplines as well as beyond academia, underscoring the importance of the close relationships where we can seek support in times of need. It is one of the cornerstones of how we understand the development of family and social relationships. It has also shaped discussions of parenting and how children are treated in medical and legal contexts. Attachment theory and research address some of the most fundamental aspects of human life, including family life, child development, intimate relationships, and the many feelings such relationships evoke.

Ideas about attachment have evolved profoundly over the 50 years since the theory was first introduced by John Bowlby. Today it is a lively area of empirical research, with numerous studies published every year, and often with surprising findings that qualify or open up classic theory in new ways. This contributes to the need for an up-to-date survey. In particular, the accumulation of research has permitted the synthesis of findings from across numerous studies (meta-analysis), which has also led to important new conclusions, regarding matters such as the role of specific adverse contexts in shaping caregiving and attachment processes.

DOI: 10.4324/9781003020349-1

The Psychology of Attachment is written to be relevant to a wide range of readers. We intend that this will include researchers and students, professionals working with adult couples, midwives, child nurses, doctors, and psychologists, preschool teachers, child protection workers, policy makers, clergy, as well as laypersons interested in child development, child-caregiver relationships, and adult romantic relationships.

The language of attachment theory and research often uses familiar terms but gives them a technical meaning. This can make it difficult for practitioners and researchers to communicate and understand one another. Misleading accounts of attachment theory and research have also entered into widespread circulation: sometimes overclaiming the significance of attachment in oversimplified terms and on the basis of single studies, sometimes dismissing it in oversimplified terms or on the basis of single studies. At other times, attachment has just been used as a buzzword when in fact there is no serious link to attachment theory or research at all.

We aim to present an account of attachment theory and research grounded in converging lines of evidence. In doing so, our goal has been to present a more accurate picture than the idealised accounts of attachment offered by some of its uncritical advocates, and the denigrating accounts of its unqualified critics. Additionally, in clarifying the meaning of terms, we aim to help make this evidence understandable, and support different communities to communicate with one another about what theory and research findings mean for them.

Despite touching on a wide range of issues, *The Psychology of Attachment* necessarily focuses on key developments. Like a tour guide showing a tourist a fascinating city, the book identifies key landmarks that offer points of orientation in the terrain. Along the way, we seek to point out areas of relative strength within attachment theory and research, as well as areas of relative weakness or current discussion among researchers.

REPORTING THE SIZE OF EFFECTS

Though there are certainly many misleading accounts of attachment theory and research about, there are also various very good introductions. In particular, we might recommend the recent book *The Science and Clinical Practice of Attachment Theory* by Allen.[1] However, these texts generally describe but do not evaluate the current state of attachment research. They also describe for the reader that attachment is associated with caregiving and with a child's later outcomes, but without specifying how much of an association. A tiny association would have a very different meaning to a very close association.

A distinctive aspect of the *The Psychology of Attachment* is how we treat research findings. We want to help the reader draw their own conclusions about the relative strength of the processes under discussion, and to avoid spurious overestimates or underestimates of the importance of caregiving and attachment for development. In particular: how strongly aspects of a child's early experience affect the quality of his or her attachment relationships, or how strongly the quality of attachment relationships affects later relationships and adjustment.

In principle, effect sizes express the extent to which one variable explains variation in another (in terms of the magnitude of a statistical coefficient). The most widely used effect size coefficient is 'r' for associations between variables. This coefficient can be either positive or negative and can range from 0 (no association) to 1 (perfect association). However, there are considerable difficulties regarding measurement in the social sciences, and tremendous complexity to human lives. The kinds of things researchers explore in the social and behavioural sciences, such as attachment, are always affected by lots of things. So reported effect sizes might be best considered as the *strength of indication that there are some important links between the phenomena of interest*, for instance between attachment relationships and later outcomes.

In this book, we have focused to a considerable degree on reports from meta-analytic research, which aggregate effect sizes from across multiple studies. Meta-analytic research is especially valuable since it offers conclusions drawn from numerous studies, and so is especially dependable knowledge. We have given this form of knowledge a degree of precedence, given the potential difficulties associated with overestimation and underestimation of the role of attachment-relevant processes. At the same time, we acknowledge that this approach also represents a limitation of our book, compared to some other works, since we give proportionately less attention to developments in theory, methodology, and research which have too few studies to support meta-analysis.

As a reference point for the reader in evaluating the strength of associations reported in this book, we include a table with various illustrations of effect sizes in social and developmental science research.

Table 0.1 *Illustrations of Effect Sizes in Social and Developmental Science Research*

Association	Effect size	Reference
Between home visiting programmes and improvements in parenting	$r = .06$	Michalopoulos et al. (2019).[2]
Between a child's readiness to show positive emotions and their success in making and maintaining friendships	$r = .10$	Borowski et al. (2021).[3]
Between interventions to reduce child maltreatment and reduction in maltreatment and related behaviours	$r = .13$	van IJzendoorn et al. (2020).[4]
Between negative life events and parents' self-reported stress	$r = .26$	Gauthier-Légaré et al. (2022).[5]
Between self-reported motivation and later school achievement	$r = .27$	Kriegbaum et al. (2018).[6]
Between socioeconomic status and academic achievement	$r = .29$	Sirin et al. (2005).[7]

CHAPTER SUMMARIES

The Psychology of Attachment comprises seven chapters and a concluding section.

In Chapter 1, we describe the background to John Bowlby's formulation of attachment theory. This includes the various theories that Bowlby drew upon in formulating attachment theory. One point we will consider carefully is what he actually meant by the term 'attachment', and we will distinguish between a 'narrow' use and a 'broad' use of the term in his work. Not just in the case of the term 'attachment', but more generally, Bowlby and subsequent attachment researchers have often given words from ordinary language technical meanings. For this reason, we have included a glossary as an appendix to this volume.

Chapter 2 details the core tenets of attachment theory as formulated by Bowlby. First, we will discuss how observations of hospitalised children in the 1940s shaped Bowlby's thinking about the importance of continuity in child-caregiver contact. The chapter outlines the typical development of attachment behaviour during the first few years of life, including how infants gradually become selective in who they direct their signalling behaviours to when distressed. We also address Bowlby's account of the role of children's expectations and trust in attachment relationships.

In Chapter 3, we focus on the work by Bowlby's close collaborator, the child psychologist Mary Ainsworth. In Uganda and the US, Ainsworth made extensive observations of infant-caregiver interactions over the first year of the infants' lives, documenting the development of individual differences in caregiving and in infants' attachment behaviour. This work, from the mid-1950s to late 1970s, led Ainsworth to important insights about the infant's use of his/her primary caregiver as a 'secure base' from which to explore and as a 'haven of safety' when distressed. Ainsworth's empirical research extended Bowlby's theory by creating a technique ('the Strange Situation procedure') for identifying individual differences in infants' organisation of attachment behaviour, which offers a window into children's expectations about their caregiver's availability and the history of the child-caregiver relationship. The chapter also explores the way Ainsworth conceptualised and measured caregiver sensitivity and child-caregiver attachment quality. The chapter also considers children's different attachment relationships and how these may become integrated into generalised expectations about others.

Chapter 4 describes research in the 1980s and early 1990s by Mary Main and colleagues on 'disorganised attachment', identified in the Strange Situation procedure by conflicted, disoriented, or apprehensive infant behaviour in the caregiver's presence. This classification has gained huge interest, in part because of associations with alarming caregiver behaviour and with child behavioural problems. After detailing the disorganised classification, we consider how disorganisation may manifest in older children in the form of controlling patterns in relation to their caregiver. The chapter also draws out the contribution of both observational and narrative assessments of individual differences in attachment for understanding children's maturation and relationships. Finally, we discuss how relevant attachment concepts and measures might be across cultures.

Chapter 5 continues the progression towards older individuals, with a focus on adults and adolescents. Cognitive development has important implications for how a child conceptualises close relationships and for how psychological processes related to attachment must be assessed. The chapter introduces an important measure introduced by Main and colleagues, the Adult Attachment Interview (AAI). The chapter describes the AAI and its different classifications, the importance of different memory systems for various types of responses, and the links between AAI classifications and adult caregivers' sensitivity to their own infants. We also look at the experience of adults who show indications in the interview that they are struggling to process experiences of loss and trauma, which is coded on the AAI with the 'unresolved' classification.

In Chapter 6, we discuss how social psychologists have used attachment theory to better understand adult personality and relationships. The chapter discusses the 'attachment styles' concept and the notion that close relationships differ along two major dimensions, anxiety and avoidance, which are usually assessed through self-report. Important correlates are discussed of anxiety and avoidance across a variety of domains. The chapter concludes with a section on adults' relationships with divine or spiritual figures. We describe research findings that suggest that humans can relate to and use their deity or deities as a secure base and safe haven.

In Chapter 7, we reflect on some important areas of focus in current attachment research. We consider 'mentalisation' and the importance of keeping babies' 'minds in mind' when caring for them. We discuss the available evidence to date of the implications of attachment for brain development. Finally, we also discuss some attachment-based interventions which have been shown to have considerable effectiveness.

In the Conclusion, we gather up the threads from the previous chapters. We return to common misconceptions about attachment and consider the reasons why these recur. We end by describing some key principles which can be taken from the convergent evidence of attachment research to date. There is also an appendix, which contains summaries of the key concepts used across the chapters, drawn from the Society for Emotion and Attachment Studies definitions.

NOTES

1 Allen, B. (2023). *The Science and Clinical Practice of Attachment Theory: A Guide from Infancy to Adulthood*. New York: APA.

2 Michalopoulos, C., Faucetta, K., Hill, C.J., Portilla, X.A., Burrell, L., Lee, H., . . . & Knox, V. (2019). *Impacts on Family Outcomes of Evidence-Based Early Childhood Home Visiting: Results from the Mother and Infant Home Visiting Program Evaluation*. Office of Planning, Research,

and Evaluation, Administration for Children and Families, U.S. Department of Health and Human Services, Washington, DC, OPRE Report 2019-07.

3 Borowski, S.K., Groh, A.M., Bakermans-Kranenburg, M.J., Fearon, P., Roisman, G.I., van IJzendoorn, M.H., & Vaughn, B.E. (2021). The significance of early temperamental reactivity for children's social competence with peers: A meta-analytic review and comparison with the role of early attachment. *Psychological Bulletin,* 147(11), 1125.

4 van IJzendoorn, M. H., Bakermans-Kranenburg, M.J., Coughlan, B., & Reijman, S. (2020). Annual research review: Umbrella synthesis of meta-analyses on child maltreatment antecedents and interventions: Differential susceptibility perspective on risk and resilience. *Journal of Child Psychology and Psychiatry,* 61(3), 272–290.

5 Gauthier-Légaré, A., Tarabulsy, G.M., Ouellet, G. et al. (2022). Exposure to negative life events and parental subjective evaluations of stress: A meta-analysis. *Journal of Child & Family Studies,* 31, 1–15.

6 Kriegbaum, K., Becker, N., & Spinath, B. (2018). The relative importance of intelligence and motivation as predictors of school achievement: A meta-analysis. *Educational Research Review,* 25, 120–148.

7 Sirin, S.R. (2005). Socioeconomic status and academic achievement: A meta-analytic review of research. *Review of Educational Research,* 75, 417–453.

1

ETHOLOGICAL-EVOLUTIONARY ATTACHMENT THEORY

FOUR SOURCES OF ATTACHMENT THEORY

1. *Psychoanalysis*: Bowlby trained as a psychoanalyst in the 1930s, attracted by the central focus it gave to the importance of family relationships for psychological development. This included the importance of family relationships for a person's emotional stability and sense of self. In psychoanalytic theory in the period, for instance in the work of Anna Freud, the term 'attachment' was used to refer to the strong value given by children to their relationship with particular caregivers, such as day care providers. This strong valuation of the relationship with a caregiver seemed to occur even if the caregiver was unkind or neglectful.

Bowlby was impressed with these aspects of psychoanalytic theory and the focus on helping children in psychoanalytic practice. However, he also had some concerns. One was the weak relationship of psychoanalytic theory to natural science. Psychoanalytic models were generated by generalising backwards about human development from close inspection of specific adult cases of mental ill health. They gained popularity through feeling relevant and evocative for practicing therapists, not by being empirically tested. In fact, many aspects of psychoanalytic theory were formulated in

DOI: 10.4324/9781003020349-2

very general, even metaphorical terms, which made them difficult, or even impossible, to test.

Another concern of Bowlby's regarding the psychoanalytic theory of his day was the underestimation of the importance of a child's actual experiences of care in shaping their development. Psychoanalysts frequently treated adult feelings of love and affection and adult mental health difficulties as resulting from a return to some early stage of development. Bowlby felt that this explanation was confused in thinking about the role of development. In his view, how adults engaged in relationships and their experience of mental health difficulties were both shaped by an individual's adaptations to their experiences over the course of their development. Bowlby thought about this in terms of an individual's 'developmental pathway': like a path, development could lead people in certain directions. But changing paths, or cutting off the path, was always possible, if sometimes more or less difficult.

Bowlby felt that many psychoanalysts placed too much emphasis on the patient's imagination – for instance, their hopes and worries about their therapist – in shaping their symptoms. Too little attention was given to what their ordinary experience was at home and how it shaped their expectations. Furthermore, some psychoanalysts placed too much emphasis on the imbalance of innate instincts. For instance, a patient facing difficulties in managing aggressive feelings could be characterised by their psychoanalyst as responding to imagined attacks by others, or as having too strong an aggressive impulse. Bowlby's impression was that therapists would do better to look at potential causes of frustration in that patient's earlier experiences.

2. *Learning theory*: In the 1960s, Bandura and colleagues developed a model of human development that emphasised learning by modelling the behaviour of others, and through feedback regarding whether a behaviour resulted in satisfaction or displeasure. This idea agreed with Bowlby's attention to the importance of actual experiences.

Whereas psychoanalytic theorists often appealed to the idea of instinct in explaining a child's care-seeking behaviours, Bowlby acknowledged that humans may be predisposed to display certain behaviours towards their caregivers, such as approaching and reaching when alarmed. However the extent, and how, these behaviours are used within the relationship with a caregiver would depend on social learning though feedback and modelling.

The importance of social learning also agreed with Bowlby's clinical work with adults who found themselves, even against their own intentions, at times repeating the actions of their parents. Yet Bowlby recognised a crucial limitation to learning theory. The theory implies that humans are just as likely to learn one behaviour as another, given particular conditions. This fails to consider the role of human evolutionary history in shaping biases to learn behaviours that may contribute to survival or reproduction. Bowlby was also critical of social learning theory for treating attachment behaviour as just a learnt response, and secondary to nutrition, whereas Bowlby saw attachment as primary, just as hunger. As both theories have subsequently developed, these sources of contention have largely been overcome.[1]

3. *Cognitive science*: Bowlby drew inspiration from cognitive science in thinking about how caregiving shapes a child's expectations about intimacy and trust. Cognitive scientists had argued that humans develop mental models based on experiences over time, and that these models are drawn upon when responding to new circumstances in the present.

Bowlby concluded that interactions with caregivers would shape how a child comes to think about and evaluate themselves and loved ones, leading over the course of development to relatively stable mental models. These models, in turn, could shape subsequent expectations or predictions about social interactions, even into adulthood. For instance, an individual's repeated experiences of caregivers as dependable or undependable could be anticipated to generate corresponding mental models. When, in later life, questions of intimacy or trust are raised by a relationship, the individual's response may well be influenced by these models, shaping the extent to which they expect others to be dependable.

Cognitive scientists had also characterised the way that our mental models filter new information. We may be more receptive to information that agrees with our existing models. This can help stabilise mental models over time, insulating them from change or re-examination, and reinforcing current assumptions. Bowlby wrote to Aaron Beck, the founder of Cognitive Behavioural Therapy, in enthusiasm for the way that Beck had given a prominent role to this filtering process. Nonetheless, Bowlby also felt that cognitive scientists, including Beck, had paid insufficient attention to the role of child development in shaping adult mental models, and had also paid insufficient attention to the defensive way that emotionally-invested mental models might differ from models about neutral facts.

Mental models elaborated in the course of interactions with caregivers during early development, Bowlby suspected, would be especially difficult to shift: the models would be embedded in taken-for-granted behaviours, and they would have shaped many aspects of a person's identity and social relationships. The strong emotions associated with these mental models would also make them difficult to reflect upon.

Nonetheless, Bowlby accepted the arguments of cognitive scientists that mental models could be abandoned if they repeatedly failed to help an individual plan for the future. Where a new model could be elaborated, the result would be a different set of assumptions about intimacy and trust. Though he felt that the old assumptions would likely lurk beneath the surface for a long time and reappear, especially when an individual is rushed into action without time to reflect.

4. *Evolutionary biology*: Even more than psychoanalysis, learning theory, and cognitive science, the most important source in Bowlby's development of attachment theory was evolutionary biology. Specifically, he was influenced by an area of study called 'ethology', which focused on the study of behavioural responses in animals and

speculation about their evolutionary basis. The revolutionary idea was that not just biological structures but also sequences of observable behaviour could be the product of evolution through natural selection.

One of the pioneers of ethology, Lorenz, had documented a 'following response' in goslings, which was directed to the first moving object the goslings encountered. This could be the goose mother. However, those goslings that were hatched in an incubator under the care of Lorenz directed their following response to him. Lorenz did not rule out that the following response could change over time. Nonetheless, he anticipated that a gosling's early exposure to a moving object would be an especially powerful influence on its subsequent following behaviour; this made the early exposure an especially critical or sensitive period.

EVOLUTION AND ETHOLOGY

Bowlby collaborated closely with the ethologist Robert Hinde in developing an account of the following response in the infants of different species. Bowlby and Hinde concluded that the following response likely evolved because it helped keep the child close to their caregivers, who could protect the child from dangers.

They anticipated that the following response would be activated in infants by feelings of alarm. This could be due to unwanted, unanticipated, or extensive separation from a familiar caregiver, which, in evolutionary history, would have represented a threat. The response could also be activated by perceptions of immediate threat. Such perceptions could be learnt by experience. However, Bowlby and Hinde anticipated that some things – like being cold, being in the dark, or loud noises – would have been primed by our evolutionary history to be experienced as alarming. In fact, in primates, the following response could incorporate clinging as further means of ensuring the caregiver's accessibility.

The experimental animal researchers Harlow and Zimmermann had used the phrase 'haven of safety' to refer to the way that an infant's alarm and motivation to seek their caregiver would be terminated once they have achieved proximity with the caregiver.[2] Bowlby and Hinde reflected that the following response could be 'terminated' or relaxed when an infant no longer felt afraid. This could occur either when the source of alarm disappeared, or when the infant perceived their familiar person or people was available as a 'safe haven'.

Familiar caregivers are therefore doubly important. Firstly, unwanted, unanticipated, or extensive separations from familiar caregivers are a source of alarm, prompting efforts to gain closeness with the caregiver. Secondly, the perceived availability of familiar caregivers is a source of reassurance, reducing feelings of alarm and relaxing the disposition to gain closeness. In the 1960s, Bowlby and Hinde agreed with Harlow and Zimmerman that access to proximity with a familiar caregiver provided a haven of safety; in the 1970s, they qualified that the perceived availability of the caregiver, at least in primates and perhaps more generally, depended on *both* the caregiver's 'accessibility' and the 'responsiveness' of the caregiver's behaviour.[3]

Hinde argued against regarding the following response as an 'instinct'. Instead he conceptualised it as a 'behavioural system': a disposition, primed by evolution, to respond to the environment in such a way as to achieve a particular goal, drawing in part on learnt experience and in part on certain behaviours disposed by the evolution of the species. Other behavioural systems included the disposition to explore new environments; the disposition to flee from things that cause alarm; the disposition to affiliate with others; the disposition to display aggression when frustrated; and the disposition to provide care to offspring. All of these behavioural systems would be shaped by experience over time to be activated and terminated, especially by particular things.

In the case of the following behavioural system, Bowlby termed the infant's differential following of particular adults and not others 'monotropy'. This term unfortunately implied that infants will select only one person – 'mono' – as the target of their care-seeking behaviour. However, for Bowlby, 'monotropy' was intended to mean a relationship to a particular person or place or thing that is personally significant, based on a felt sense of need, and not superficial or interchangeable with other people, places, or things even if they are somewhat similar.

Of particular interest to Hinde and Bowlby was the observation that the same person, place, or thing could be the target for more than one behavioural system. Hinde conducted extensive observations of chaffinches and was interested in the way that sexual, aggressive, and fear responses could be seen when a male and female approached each other. Where behavioural systems were incompatible – one requiring the individual to approach, another requiring the individual to avoid or flee – the birds displayed behaviours expressing this contradiction.

These 'conflict behaviours' included alternation of one kind of behaviour, then the other; contradictory displays of both behaviours at the same time; misdirected movements; stress movements; or stopping in place for a time, displaying neither form of behaviour. Bowlby was fascinated by the analogies between these conflict behaviours and many of the symptoms he had seen as a clinician working with combat veterans, as a family therapist, and in observations of hospitalised children experiencing long-term separations from their parents. As we will see in Chapter 4, Hinde's account of conflict behaviours would also form the basis for the idea of disorganised attachment.

ATTACHMENT THEORY

Bowlby's attachment theory combines, as discussed above, ideas and methods from various other theoretical perspectives. This contributed to some of the theory's special strengths. The concept of 'attachment' was taken from Anna Freud's account of the value children put on relationships with caregivers, and was fused with Hinde's characterisation of the following behavioural system. Hinde did not approve: he thought that using the term 'attachment' in this way would confuse people.

Yet there were advantages for Bowlby to such a mix of psychoanalytic and ethological ideas within a single term. On the one hand, it gave the ethological concept of 'following' a deeper emotional resonance, helping to retain some portion of the recognition of children's rich inner life foregrounded by psychoanalysis. On the other hand, it gave a psychoanalytic model greater specification, directing attention to children's efforts to achieve the availability of their caregiver when alarmed.

This established the basis for attachment theory as an empirical paradigm, one that emphasised the centrality of children's day-to-day experiences of interaction with familiar caregivers. Bowlby's perspective also generated predictions regarding the importance of early child-caregiver relationships for the child's expectations about the availability of others in times of need, and the importance of these expectations for that child's subsequent development. This perspective also highlighted the difficulties that could be caused by serious disruptions to a child's perception of the availability of a safe haven.

However, as a result of Bowlby's merger of psychoanalytic and ethological ideas, the term 'attachment' ended up, quite confusingly, with both narrow and broad meanings in his writings:

- Narrowly, attachment could mean the following response and related actions that serve to monitor and maintain access to the caregiver, integrating social learning about the effectiveness of different care-seeking behaviours.
- Broadly, the same term could mean an emotionally-invested relationship, available as a concrete or symbolic source of comfort, and a filter on new information relevant to intimacy and trust.

The narrow term is technical, whereas the broad meaning is closer to the ordinary language use of the term 'attachment'. Bowlby shuttled between these distinct meanings, rarely clarifying for his reader.

For example, in Bowlby's writings, 'attachment' was sometimes used broadly to mean emotionally-invested relationships as a whole. With this meaning in mind, in the 1950s, he would sometimes, confusingly, write about parents being 'attached' to their child. He had abandoned this usage by the 1960s. However, he continued frequently to use the term 'attachment' to broadly mean emotionally invested relationships. Late in his career, with the broad meaning in mind, Bowlby argued that "attachments to other human beings are the hub around which a person's life revolves. . . . From these intimate attachments a person draws his strength and enjoyment of life."[4] Such claims would contribute to the misapprehension that individual differences in early attachment are fixed for life. This was likely supported by a tendency in Bowlby's writings, inherited from psychoanalysis, to treat infant-caregiver interaction as a model and metaphor for all human emotion regulation and relating. This would also be consequential for later attachment research, including the work of Mary Main, as we shall see in Chapters 3 and 4.

On the other hand, when 'attachment' was understood narrowly as a specific behavioural system, Bowlby's stance was rather different. With the narrow ethological meaning in mind, he argued that parents are absolutely not 'attached' to their child, since, in the narrow sense, the child is not primarily the target of the parent's following response; instead, the parent provides care to the child. That is, he viewed child-caregiver attachment relationships as hierarchical, with children (the weaker parts), following and seeking care from their caregivers (the stronger parts), since this had presumably promoted children's chances of survival. He also tended towards more qualified claims about the impact of early attachment. The period of early following and help-seeking has its importance because "the period when they are most active is also the period when patterns of control and of regulating conflict are being laid down".[5] Yet even children who have had "ghastly experiences" may "nevertheless develop favourably", with – he predicted – maybe only 20–30% subsequently showing severe problems.[6] Any one factor, including early experiences of care, which he saw as foundational, would at most repeatedly influence, not determine, developmental pathways.

From the 1970s, Bowlby expressed regret in correspondence with colleagues that he had used Anna Freud's term 'attachment' at all, since so many people got confused between the broad and narrow meanings. Hinde had been right about the dangers of the term. Bowlby wished that he had used the term 'care-seeking' instead. However he sensed it was too late to change things as the concept of attachment had already entered into circulation.

In his 1980 book *Loss*, Bowlby provided a summary of attachment theory.[7] This summary conveys a strong sense of Bowlby as a thinker and how he conceptualised child development and relationships. It is also a passage in his work that is more conceptually exact in using the term 'attachment' than some of his earlier writings, which is helpful for understanding his meaning:

a) Attachment behaviour is conceived as any form of behaviour that results in a person attaining or retaining proximity to some other differentiated and preferred individual. So long as the attachment figure remains accessible and responsive the behaviour may consist of little more than checking by eye or ear on the whereabouts of the figure and exchanging occasional glances and greetings. In certain circumstances, however, following or clinging to the attachment figure may occur and also calling or crying, which are likely to elicit his or her caregiving.

b) As a class of behaviour with its own dynamic, attachment behaviour is conceived as distinct from feeding behaviour and sexual behaviour and of at least an equal significance in human life.

c) During the course of healthy development attachment behaviour leads to the development of affectional bonds or attachments, initially between child and parent and later between adult and adult. The forms of behaviour and the bonds to which they lead are present and active throughout the life cycle (and by no means confined to childhood as other theories assume).

d) The goal of attachment behaviour is to maintain certain degrees of proximity to, or of communication with, the discriminated attachment figure(s).

e) Whereas an attachment bond endures . . . attachment behaviour are activated only by certain conditions, for example strangeness, fatigue, anything frightening, and unavailability or unresponsiveness of attachment figure, and are terminated only by certain other conditions, for example a familiar environment and the ready availability and responsiveness of an attachment figure.

f) Many of the most intense emotions arise during the formation, the maintenance, the disruption and the renewal of attachment relationships. The formation of a bond is described as falling in love, maintaining a bond as loving someone, and losing a partner as grieving over someone. Similarly, threat of loss arouses anxiety and actual loss gives rise to sorrow; while each of these situations is likely to arouse anger. The unchallenged maintenance of a bond is experienced as a source of security and the renewal of a bond as a source of joy. Because such emotions are usually a reflection of the state of a person's affectional bonds, the psychology and psychopathology of emotion is found to be in large part the psychology and psychopathology of affectional bonds.

g) Attachment behaviour has become a characteristic of many species during the course of their evolution because it contributes to the individual's survival by keeping him in touch with his caregiver(s), thereby reducing the risk of his coming to harm, for example from cold, hunger or drowning and, in man's environment of evolutionary adaptedness, especially from predators.

h) Behaviour complementary to attachment behaviour and serving a complementary function, that of protecting the attached individual, is caregiving. This is commonly shown by a parent, or other adult, towards a child or adolescent, but is also shown by one adult towards another, especially in times of ill health, stress or old age.

i) In view of attachment behaviour being potentially active throughout life and also of its having the vital biological function proposed, it is held a grave error to suppose that, when active in an adult, attachment behaviour is indicative either of pathology or of regression to immature behaviour.

j) Psychopathology is regarded as due to a person's psychological development having followed a deviant pathway, and not as due to his suffering a fixation at, or a regression to, some early stage of development.

k) Disturbed patterns of attachment behaviour can be present at any age due to development having followed a deviant pathway. One of the commonest forms of disturbance is the over-ready elicitation of attachment behaviour, resulting in anxious attachment. Another . . . is a partial or complete deactivation of attachment behaviour.

l) Principal determinants of the pathway along which an individual's attachment behaviour develops, and of the pattern in which it becomes organised, are the experiences he has with his attachment figures during his years of immaturity – infancy, childhood and adolescence.

Some of the fundamental strengths of Bowlby's ideas will be shown over the subsequent chapters. Not least, researchers have documented links over time between a child's early care and their later behaviour and mental health (Chapters 3 and 4). They have also used the model of the care-seeking infant as a lens on adult mental processing and functioning in relationships (Chapters 5 and 6). There is a great deal in Bowlby's ideas that remains tremendously relevant and exciting. In our view, this includes the specific importance he gave to the experience of trust in the availability of a safe haven in times of need, which is an insight with diverse potential applications.

Yet Bowlby's theory also incorporated weaknesses from its constituent parts. A first set of weaknesses stemmed from the way that the constituent disciplines got trapped in amber. Developments in evolutionary biology and cognitive science after the 1970s, in particular, failed to penetrate Bowlby's thinking or – with exceptions – the work of most later attachment researchers. For instance, the concept of the attachment behavioural system has not seen update in light of subsequent work in evolutionary biology. This is in contrast, for instance, to the cognitive science used by Bowlby, which has been updated by later attachment researchers (Chapter 5).

A second set of weaknesses stemmed from limitations in the constituent disciplines themselves. Bowlby's approach remained psychoanalytic in key regards, not least that some conclusions were often based on a few clinical cases rather than the empirical testing of hypotheses. Bowlby also retained from psychoanalysis a tendency to claim a direct relationship between early childhood and later mental health, without qualification or interaction with other factors. Bowlby often failed to consider the role of moderators and mediators of the effects of early experience on child development:

- Moderators: factors that change the strength of a relationship between two variables or indicate *when* exactly a particular effect can be anticipated.
- Mediators: factors that specify *how* or explain *why* a particular relationship exists between two variables.

For instance, Bowlby underappreciated the role of cultural and communal processes involved in the care of children, including the potential for children to have care-seeking relationships with multiple people. He neglected attention to the role of culture in moderating and mediating children's experiences of care. Furthermore, in taking a cross-species perspective, Bowlby tended to downplay features relatively more characteristic of humans, such as the role of higher cognition. His ideas displayed an overemphasis on protection at the expense of other potential functions of a child's following and valuing a familiar caregiver, such as learning. We will revisit these weaknesses in Bowlby's thinking in the subsequent chapters.

Table 1.1 Disciplines Integrated by Bowlby in the Development of Attachment Theory

Discipline	Strengths	Weaknesses
British psychoanalysis (c.1950s)	• Recognition that even young children have a rich inner life • Recognition of the strong value given by children to their relationships with particular caregivers, even if these caregivers are unkind or neglectful	• Questionable relation to natural science • Emphasis on fantasy at the expense of the importance of actual childhood experiences • Theory of instincts • Use of infancy as a model and metaphor for all human emotion regulation and social relationships
Learning theory (c.1960s)	• Recognition of the importance of actual experiences • Recognition of the importance of feedback and modelling as developmental processes	• Overemphasis on plasticity of learnt responses • Underemphasis on evolutionary processes in predisposing certain behaviours
Cognitive science (c.1950s–1970s)	• Recognition of the role of filtering of new information on the basis of expectations	• Insufficient attention to child development in giving certain cognitions special importance • Insufficient attention to emotions and defences in giving certain cognitions special importance
Evolutionary biology (c.1950s–1960s)	• Provided cross-species observations of juvenile following behaviour • Identified that the nature and target of certain behaviours may be shaped especially in particular periods of development	• In looking at cross-species, tended to downplay features specific to humans, such as the role of higher cognition

Discipline	Strengths	Weaknesses
	• Recognition that various behaviours could be used to satisfy the same motivation • Recognition that the terminating conditions of the following response would be discriminated to particular, familiar figures, places, or things • Meticulous documentation of 'conflict behaviours', which occur when two responses are incompatible	• Overemphasis on protection at the expense of other potential functions of a child's following and valuing a familiar caregiver, such as learning • Insufficient attention to communal processes in the care of infants

NOTES

1 Bosmans, G., Bakermans-Kranenburg, M.J., Vervliet, B., Verhees, M.W., & van IJzendoorn, M.H. (2020). A learning theory of attachment: Unraveling the black box of attachment development. *Neuroscience & Biobehavioral Reviews*, 113, 287–298.

2 Harlow, H.F., & Zimmermann, R.R. (1958). The development of affectional responses in infant monkeys. *Proceedings of the American Philosophical Society*, 102(5), 501–509.

3 Bowlby, J. (1973). *Separation: Anxiety and Anger*. New York: Basic Books, p. 234.

4 Bowlby, J. (1980). *Loss*. London: Pimlico, p. 442.

5 Bowlby, J. (1960). Separation anxiety. *International Journal of Psycho-Analysis*, 41, 89–113, p. 105.

6 Bowlby, J. (1986). Interview with the BBC. Wellcome Collection, John Bowlby Archive, PP/Bow/F.5/8.

7 Bowlby, J. (1980). *Loss*. London: Pimlico, pp. 38–40.

FURTHER RECOMMENDED READING

Bowlby, J. (1991). Ethological light on psychoanalytic problems. In P. Bateson (Ed.), *The Development and Integration of Behaviour: Essays in Honour of Robert Hinde* (pp. 301–314). Cambridge: Cambridge University Press.

Duschinsky, R. (2020). John Bowlby and the Tavistock separation research unit. In *Cornerstones of Attachment Research*. Oxford: Oxford University Press.

Granqvist, P. (2021). Attachment, culture, and gene-culture co-evolution: Expanding the evolutionary toolbox of attachment theory. *Attachment & Human Development, 23*(1), 90–113.

Thompson, R.A., Simpson, J.A., & Berlin, L.J. (Eds.). (2021). *Attachment: The Fundamental Questions*. New York: Guilford.

2

THE NORMATIVE TENETS OF ATTACHMENT THEORY

SEPARATION

Bowlby wanted to demonstrate the importance of actual experiences of care, and continuity of such care, for children's mental health. In the 1940s, he therefore reported case histories from his work at a child guidance clinic. These case histories suggested that early separation experiences might predispose later conduct problems by disrupting the bases of a child's self-worth and capacity for empathy. Bowlby suspected that other early adversities and maltreatment could also have relevant effects. Yet, he concluded that separations would be easier to document, to help make the basic case for the importance of early childhood experiences and for the importance of sufficiently continuous access to care from familiar caregivers.

At the time, it was common policy to keep parents from visiting their children in the hospital. Bowlby therefore embarked upon a study of children undergoing hospitalisation. He hired James Robertson, a social worker who had previously worked with Anna Freud, to conduct observations of around 50 children at the hospital and, where possible, on reunion with their parents. He also hired Mary Ainsworth, a Canadian clinical psychologist, to help analyse the observations.

DOI: 10.4324/9781003020349-3

As part of this research, Robertson made a film, *A Two-Year-Old Goes to Hospital*. The film documented the behaviour of Laura, a little girl who was hospitalised for eight days without visits from her family. This film showed Laura's intense distress and preoccupation with her caregiver following separation, and the withdrawn behaviours that followed. The distinction between anxious preoccupation and withdrawn behaviours intrigued the research team. In a paper from 1956 reporting on their follow-up study with the hospitalised children, Bowlby, Ainsworth, and colleagues wrote that "the personality patterns of children who have experienced long separation tend to fall into one or other of these two opposite classes": either "mother-rejecting . . . having repressed their need for attachment", or "over-dependent" and "ambivalent".[1] Bowlby theorised that the withdrawn behaviours stemmed from an inhibition of the attachment behavioural system, as children despaired of achieving reunion with their caregivers.

Bowlby's focus on documentable separations was successful in drawing clinical, research, and public attention. However, in certain regards, the strategy backfired. In the 1950s, Bowlby generally documented separations as either *present* or *absent*. This crude measure had high reliability. Anyone could check the record and would agree whether there had been a separation or not. Unfortunately this methodology contributed to a tendency for Bowlby to think and write about separations as merely present or absent, at least until the early 1970s. Kinds of separations were not distinguished. Bowlby used the term 'separation' to connote everything from a child sleeping alone in a room, to use of day care, to child neglect, to institutionalisation in an orphanage.

Bowlby's central theoretical interest was in major separations, lasting weeks or months. However, his imprecise discussions of 'separation' gave the impression that caregivers, and specifically mothers, should always be physically present for their children. This was not a view that Bowlby himself stated after the 1950s. His private notes and correspondence indicate that he was baffled that it was attributed to him. In retrospect, it is not especially surprising: he had not done enough to clarify what he meant by 'separations' in his published writings.

Bowlby was right that separations can be harmful, if they convey to the child that they lack a familiar caregiver who they can turn to when alarmed. The clearest case is institutional care, in which children are looked after by a rotating set of adult professionals, which is associated with a wide array of negative outcomes.[2] Where a child lacks the experience of an accessible and responsive familiar caregiver, as a result of severe parental neglect, this is also consequential, and some research suggests it has the most significant impact of any form of child maltreatment.[3]

Only if day care is very extensive (over 70 hours a week) for young children do attachment researchers generally find indications of disruption of the attachment behavioural system, perhaps because the child is unable to sustain a sense of the caregiver's availability.[4] But not all day care has this effect. For instance, longitudinal research in the United States following 1,153 children from infancy to adolescence found that quality day care for children whose mothers were facing life stresses conferred a net benefit rather than a risk.[5]

THE DEVELOPMENT OF ATTACHMENT

Children are not born with a functioning attachment behavioural system. Infants only gradually identify particular figures as the targets for attachment behaviour. Although much research on neonates has since shown that they have a clearer preference for their familiar caregivers (e.g., those individuals' voices, their smell) over unfamiliar interaction partners than Bowlby realised, it usually takes more than six to seven months before what appears as full-fledged attachment relationship with caregivers has been established ("prototypical attachment," in Bowlby's words). The attachment system is only really functionally operational from the second half of a child's first year. This process depends in part on sufficient cognitive maturation but also on sufficient experience of interaction.

During the second half of the first year of life, a child is likely to show increasing preference for familiar caregivers, coupled with separation anxiety when parted from those caregivers and wariness to interacting with strangers. Although the intensity of expressions of separation anxiety and stranger wariness are notably variable across children and cultures – in part due to temperamental factors and cultural caregiving practices – both phenomena are strongly normative (i.e., species-typical), indeed probably universal. Attachment formation also coalesces with infants' increased physical mobility (as evident in crawling and walking) and cognitive developments, most notably object permanence (i.e., the understanding that an object, such as the caregiver, will continue to exist even when not perceptibly present). Jointly, these developing motoric and cognitive abilities enable infants not just to actively seek proximity to their caregivers and to search for them when they are absent (such as during a brief separation) but also to venture off into potentially dangerous territories. At this age, the attachment system kicks into high gear and becomes visibly functional. Much of the infant-toddler's life – at roughly 9 to 18 months of age – is subsequently organised around establishing and maintaining reasonable proximity to attachment figures while also exploring the surrounding world with its appealing objects and settings, using the caregiver as a secure base.

When children are around 3–5 years old, their relationships with attachment figures gain increased flexibility and depth. This happens because of repeated interaction sequences corroborating the child's models of self and other but also because of increased language abilities and further cognitive developments, including mentalisation (Chapter 7). The child now has a set of expectations that in most situations, such as during separations in familiar settings, there is no need to resort to overt attachment behaviours (such as crying or following) because of an internalised representation of the attachment figure as someone who 'plans' or 'intends' to come back and who 'cares about' how the child is feeling.

Where a younger child more frequently needs the attachment figure's actual presence, a preschool-aged or older child may be able to take

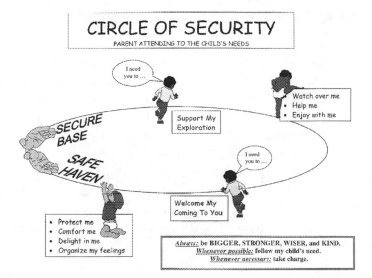

Figure 2.1 Characterisation of how children maintain proximity to their attachment figures, and approach them as safe havens for comfort and protection, while simultaneously using them as secure bases from which they explore the surrounding world. The attachment figure is depicted by the leftmost hands, and important caregiver behaviours are noted.

Source: The figure, reprinted with permission, comes from the intervention program Circle of Security (Marvin et al., 2002)[6]

comfort in expectations and representations built up from past experiences, which Bowlby termed as the child's "internalised secure base". The child can now more easily endure somewhat longer separations.

The preschooler can also engage in mind-related conversations with its caregivers (and others), which has the potential to expand the child's understanding of self and others and to facilitate relational repair when things have temporarily gone sour. Such conversations can effectively restore the child's sense of confidence in the parent's accessibility, the self's continued worthiness of care, and the good intentions of the parent's mind. Because of the increased flexibility of the relationship that ensues, Bowlby referred to this phase of attachment relationship development as the "goal-corrected partnership."

ONE ATTACHMENT FIGURE OR MANY

Beyond attachment to a parent or other principal caregiver, Bowlby and Ainsworth identified that the attachment behavioural system will likely also have other targets who can be sought by someone when they are alarmed. Bowlby discussed attachment to other family members, such as grandparents and to psychotherapists. If these individuals are sufficiently familiar to the person, they may be sought as a safe haven when the person is alarmed, and used as a secure base for exploration. Familiarity is however important, as the person needs time to develop expectations about the other individual's accessibility and responsiveness for potentially providing a safe haven and secure base. Sufficient continuity of contact is also important for the person to be able to maintain such expectancies on the other individual. Perhaps for these reasons, there is still very limited research on attachment to other family members, such as grandparents and siblings.

Bowlby sometimes also speculated that non-human entities, such as one's home or divine beings, can function as targets of the attachment behavioural system, where they are experienced as available and receptive under conditions of alarm. Ultimately, there remained some ambiguity in Bowlby's thinking about what exactly constitutes an attachment relationship.

Later attachment researchers have highlighted that various figures may serve as attachment figures for children. However, they have agreed with Bowlby that for children to perceive at least one familiar human caregiver as available in times of need will be fundamental to human socioemotional development. Yet a major limitation of attachment research as a paradigm has been the powerful tendency of researchers to focus empirical studies on the infant's relationship with his or her mother. This is largely based on the choice by researchers to examine the caregiving relationship most familiar to the child, which is the mother for most infants in most cultures. A focus on mothers also more easily allows researchers to place new findings in conversation with the existing literature. Pragmatically, mothers have also been much easier to recruit.

Despite this empirical overemphasis on mother-child relationships, attachment researchers believe that all regular targets for the attachment behavioural system are important. The idea of attachment relationships as forming a 'network' for the child has been fundamental for contemporary attachment researchers. The safe haven provision provided by one member of a child's network has been found in general to be only moderately related to the safe haven provision provided by another.[7] Though the extent of convergence and divergence will depend on a variety of cultural and social factors, access to a network of attachment figures can nonetheless be anticipated to generally increase the likelihood that a child will have someone they can feel confident turning to in times of need. In turn, the support for childcare provided by additional network members, for instance, grandparents, can increase the capacity of individuals within the network to provide a safe haven for children when needed.[8]

The importance of the attachment network is also demonstrated by empirical findings. There are specific benefits to a secure attachment network over and above a single secure attachment relationship with a primary caregiver. Dagan and colleagues used meta-analysis to synthesise results across studies and found that children with two secure attachment relationships in infancy later had fewer behavioural difficulties and stronger language skills than those with either one or no secure attachment relationship.[9] In our view, this is one of the most exciting areas in contemporary attachment research.

Though all contemporary attachment researchers agree in principle with the idea of an attachment network, some still believe that infants are evolutionarily primed to treat their most familiar caregiver as of special importance. However, whether infants treat a particular caregiver as of special importance for a time is a separate matter to the relative contribution of different early attachment relationships to later psychological development.[10] Recent meta-analytic research has found that the safe haven provision of fathers and mothers, for instance, has similar influence on a child's later behavioural development.[11]

If more than one caregiver is available, an alarmed child tends to seek out the currently most familiar person.[12] However one attachment relationship is not at the expense of another. As Ainsworth put it: "a child cared for by several caregivers can, and frequently does, form as secure an attachment to one figure, his mother, as a child who has a more exclusive relationship with one figure".[13]

An exception is when an individual spends insufficient time with a child to be experienced as familiar, and for expectations about availability to develop for the child. Bowlby criticised institutions that would allow children to go for a long time without seeing their familiar caregivers, such as residential nurseries. However, he readily acknowledged that children can form attachments to day care providers if the staff-to-child ratio and staff turnover are not too high. These staff may then be sought when the child is distressed in the nursery or preschool context. As we saw in the previous chapter, the very term 'attachment' was taken from Anna Freud's observations in her nursery. Bowlby held that children would experience distress whenever an unwanted, unanticipated, or extensive separation occurred within the most important attachment relationships. However, other relationships can function as attachments to the extent that they are looked for as a safe haven.

A difficulty in understanding Bowlby's claims here lies in the fact that different kinds of separation – including day care – were not well distinguished. Bowlby also frequently used the term 'mother' to mean any attachment relationship, following standard psychoanalytic language in his day. He has been widely and rightly criticised for this, including by close colleagues like Mary Ainsworth.[14] Feminist critics have observed that Bowlby's statements about the dangers of separation were taken up by policymakers to argue against progressive family policies, such as subsidised nurseries for children.[15] In his works from the 1970s and 1980s, Bowlby clarified his claims about separation and the defining characteristics of attachment relationships. However, these were written for a scientific audience, and the technical and abstract language made it difficult for these subsequent qualifications to rectify early errors and ambiguities.

Bowlby was begged by colleagues to write something for a popular audience stating his view that it was not nurseries in general that
were harmful to children but residential nurseries where children
may not see their families for several days or longer. However, he
focused his energies on writing scholarly, not popular work from the
1970s. In his letters and private notes, he appeared genuinely sur-
prised that people thought he was wholly critical of the use of day
care, apparently having forgotten his earlier statements. Yet in failing
to engage with questions of policy and practical child welfare in
his theoretical writings, Bowlby missed opportunities for conceptual
specification. For instance, greater consideration of the safe haven
provision offered by day care staff could have helped Bowlby get
more specific about the processes, besides familiarity, that lead to the
selection of people (or places or things) as targets of the attachment
behavioural system.

A lack of precision in Bowlby's thinking about multiple care
arrangements led to a breakdown of communication with anthropologist critics of his work. In discussions at the World Health
Organization in the 1950s, the anthropologist Margaret Mead told
Bowlby that, in her view, a child would do perfectly well with 20
different caregivers. Bowlby replied that he did not think having
multiple caregivers would cause harm to a child by any means. It
would depend on the nature of the care. Roughly equal care by
20 caregivers would run the risk that none would be sufficiently
familiar for the child to be able to develop expectations about their
availability as a safe haven.

This argument has subsequently been supported by research with
children in institutional care, as we saw earlier. The high staff-to-
child ratio and staff turnover make it much harder for a child in
the institution to experience a particular caregiver as a safe haven.
Anthropologists have themselves subsequently observed that "even
in contexts of multiple caregiving, infants generally do not form
close relationships with more than a few individuals."[16] It is clear
that children can develop multiple attachment relationships, and
that sufficient opportunities for developing expectations on the

caregivers' accessibility and responsivity is key. Yet, it is unclear if children's attachment networks have a maximum size, and whether cognitive development play a role in enabling an increasingly larger network.

Unfortunately, however, Bowlby's impression of what was meant when anthropologists spoke of "multiple caregiving arrangements" was frozen at Mead's characterisation of twenty interchangeable people. The result was that Bowlby neglected discussion of the role of multi-adult interactions. This has had a variety of consequences for attachment research. Perhaps the most important has been that no designated space was given in his model of the attachment system for the role of communal and cultural factors in shaping or scaffolding the manner with which infants utilise caregivers as a safe haven.[17]

Though there have been exceptions,[18] Bowlby's legacy has contributed to a relative neglect of the issue of communal institutions and of culture in the theorising and development of measures among subsequent attachment researchers, at least until relatively recently. This includes neglect of the positive contributions communal institutions and culture may make to people's experience of the availability of others in times of need, as well as the negative contributions communal institutions and culture may make, for instance, through the effects of racism and oppression.[19]

NOTES

1 Bowlby, J., Ainsworth, M., Boston, M., & Rosenbluth, D. (1956). The effects of mother-child separation: A follow-up study. *British Journal of Medical Psychology*, 29, 211–247, p. 238.

2 Van IJzendoorn, M.H., Bakermans-Kranenburg, M.J., Duschinsky, R., Goldman, P.S., Fox, N.A., Gunnar, M.R., Johnson, D.E., Nelson, C.A., Reijman, S., Skinner, G.C.M., Zeanah, C.H., & Sonuga-Barke, E.J.S. (2020). The impact of institutionalisation and deinstitutionalisation on children's development – a systematic and integrative review of evidence from across the globe. *Lancet Child & Adolescent Health*, 7(8), 703–720.

3 Mbagaya, C., Oburu, P., & Bakermans-Kranenburg, M.J. (2013). Child physical abuse and neglect in Kenya, Zambia and the Netherlands: A cross-cultural comparison of prevalence, psychopathological sequelae and mediation by PTSS. *International Journal of Psychology*, 48(2), 95–107.

4 Hazen, N.L., Allen, S.D., Christopher, C.H., Umemura, T., & Jacobvitz, D.B. (2015). Very extensive nonmaternal care predicts mother – infant attachment disorganization: Convergent evidence from two samples. *Development & Psychopathology*, 27(3), 649–661.

5 NICHD Early Child Care Research Network. (1997). The effects of infant child care on infant – mother attachment security. *Child Development*, 68(5), 860–879.

6 Marvin, R., Cooper, G., Hoffman, K., & Powell, B. (2002). The circle of security project: Attachment-based intervention with caregiver-pre-school child dyads. *Attachment & Human Development*, 4(1), 107–124.

7 Ahnert, L., Pinquart, M., & Lamb, M.E. (2006). Security of children's relationships with nonparental care providers: A meta-analysis. *Child Development*, 77(3), 664–679; Deneault, A.A., Cabrera, N.J., & Bureau, J.F. (2022). A meta-analysis on observed paternal and maternal sensitivity. *Child Development*, 93(6), 1631–1648.

8 Liang, X., Lin, Y., Van IJzendoorn, M.H., & Wang, Z. (2021). Grandmothers are part of the parenting network, too! A longitudinal study on coparenting, maternal sensitivity, child attachment and behavior problems in a Chinese sample. *New Directions for Child and Adolescent Development*, 2021(180), 95–116.

9 Dagan, O., Schuengel, C., Verhage, M.L., van IJzendoorn, M.H., Sagi-Schwartz, A., Madigan, S., . . . Collaboration on Attachment to Multiple Parents and Outcomes Synthesis. (2021). Configurations of mother-child and father-child attachment as predictors of internalizing and externalizing behavioral problems: An individual participant data (IPD) meta-analysis. *New Directions for Child and Adolescent Development*, 2021(180), 67–94; Dagan, O., et al. (2022). Configurations of mother-child and father-child attachment as predictors of child language competence: An individual participant data meta-analysis. https://psyarxiv.com/ts4hq/download?format=pdf

10 Dagan, O., & Sagi-Schwartz, A. (2018). Early attachment network with mother and father: An unsettled issue. *Child Development Perspectives*, 12(2), 115–121.

11 Cooke, J.E., Deneault, A.-A., Devereaux, C., Eirich, R., Fearon, R.M.P., & Madigan, S. (2022). Parental sensitivity and child behavioral problems: A meta-analytic review. *Child Development*, 93(5), 1231–1248.

12 Umemura, T., Jacobvitz, D., Messina, S., & Hazen, N. (2013). Do toddlers prefer the primary caregiver or the parent with whom they feel more secure? The role of toddler emotion. *Infant Behavior and Development*, 36(1), 102–114.

13 Ainsworth, M. (1963). The development of infant–mother interaction among the Ganda. In B.M. Foss (Ed.), *Determinants of Infant Behaviour*, vol. 2 (pp. 67–104). London: Methuen, p. 95.

14 Ainsworth, M. (1962). The effects of maternal deprivation: A review of findings and controversy in the context of research strategy. In *Deprivation of Maternal Care: A Reassessment of Its Effects* (pp. 87–195). Geneva: WHO, p. 101.

15 Lewis, J. (2013). The failure to expand childcare provision and to develop a comprehensive childcare policy in Britain during the 1960s and 1970s. *Twentieth Century British History*, 24(2), 249–274.

16 Harkness, S. (2015). The strange situation of attachment research: A review of three books. *Reviews in Anthropology*, 44(3), 178–197, p. 196.

17 Schmidt, W.J., Keller, H., & Rosabal Coto, M. (2021). Development in context: What we need to know to assess children's attachment relationships. *Developmental Psychology*, 57(12), 2206–2219.

18 Posada, G., Jacobs, A., Richmond, M., Carbonell, O., Alzate, G., Bustamante, M., & Quiceno, J. (2002). Maternal caregiving and infant security in two cultures. *Developmental Psychology*, 38(1), 67–78.

19 Causadias, J.M., Morris, K.S., Cárcamo, R.A., Neville, H.A., Nóblega, M., Salinas-Quiroz, F., & Silva, J.R. (2022). Attachment research and anti-racism: Learning from Black and Brown scholars. *Attachment & Human Development*, 24(3), 366–372.

FURTHER RECOMMENDED READING

Bakermans-Kranenburg, M.J. (2021). The limits of the attachment network. *New Directions for Child and Adolescent Development*, 2021(180), 117–124.

Bowlby, J. (1973). *Separation: Anxiety and Anger*. New York: Basic Books.

Dagan, O., & Sagi-Schwartz, A. (2018). Early attachment network with mother and father: An unsettled issue. *Child Development Perspectives*, 12(2), 115–121.

Marvin, R.S., Britner, A.A., & Russell, B.A. (2016). Normative development: The ontogeny of attachment in childhood. In J. Cassidy & P.R. Shaver (Eds.), *Handbook of Attachment: Theory, Research, and Clinical Applications*, 3rd ed. (pp. 273–290). New York: Guilford.

3

INDIVIDUAL DIFFERENCES IN INFANT ATTACHMENT PATTERNS

SECURITY AND SENSITIVITY

In 1953, Ainsworth left Bowlby's research group in London to move to Kampala, Uganda, where her husband had been appointed to a job at the East Africa Institute of Social Research. Ainsworth received funding from the Institute for an ethnographic study of caregiving in Uganda. A decade later in Baltimore, she built upon this work in a longitudinal study of 26 mother–infant dyads throughout the first year of life. Described in her classic work, *Patterns of Attachment*, this study generated some of the most innovative and influential ideas and methods in developmental psychology.

Ainsworth was interested in the way some children appeared to have greater trust in the accessibility and responsiveness of their caregiver. She termed this 'security'. In her data, these children seemed to display greater confidence in their caregiver as a haven of safety when they were alarmed, and could be comforted more easily. They also seemed to explore more freely, using the caregiver as a 'secure base', with less apparent anxiety about whether the caregiver would be available. Ainsworth's students would later term an individual's subjective sense of confidence in their caregivers as 'felt security',

DOI: 10.4324/9781003020349-4

or as a 'secure base script'. Attachment security has been found to predict later outcomes, with robust, if moderate, associations with measures such as social competence $(r = .19)$[1] and growth in self-esteem over time $(r = .19)$.[2]

Something to be aware of is that the term 'security' was used by Ainsworth in a technical sense, rather different from how the word is used in everyday language. In fact, Ainsworth intended the term security to mean confidence in the other's accessibility and responsiveness. Furthermore, in considering how the kind of caregiving a child received might impact this confidence, Ainsworth did not mean to imply that caregiving would be the only source of security. In fact, Ainsworth argued, we may draw feelings of security from many sources (e.g, the larger community, a society's welfare system).

Nonetheless, her empirical study was of parenting behaviours, and her observations suggested that a child's confidence in their primary caregiver as a haven of safety and secure base was linked to particular kinds of caregiver behaviour. Ainsworth identified four components of what she called caregiver 'interactive behaviours', so called because they could only be identified in relation to the baby's behaviour. Examples of interactive behaviours included, for example, noticing the baby's facial expressions, facilitating exploration by placing a toy within reach, or responding expressively when the infant did something engaging. Ainsworth developed scales to capture four facets of mother's interactive behaviour: sensitivity (vs. insensitivity) to signals, cooperation (vs. interference) with the infant's ongoing behaviour; acceptance (vs. rejection) of the infant's needs, and physical/psychological availability (vs. unavailability).

In Ainsworth's sample, these scales had a close relationship with one another. She gave particular prominence to the scale for sensitivity vs. insensitivity. Ainsworth defined sensitivity as the ability of the caregiver to "perceive and to interpret accurately the signals and communications implicit in her infant's behaviour, and given this understanding, to respond to them appropriately and promptly".[3] This response need not be to follow the child's apparent wishes; rather the caregiver "acknowledges the baby's wishes even though she does not unconditionally accede to them", since much of what is "for the baby's own good is done contrary to his wishes." Here is Ainsworth's characterisation of the highly sensitive care in her scale:

Highly sensitive: This mother is exquisitely attuned to B's signals; and responds to them promptly and appropriately. She is able to see things from B's point of view; her perceptions of his signals and communications are not distorted by her own needs and defenses. She "reads" B's signals and communications skillfully, and knows what the meaning is of even his subtle, minimal, and understated cue. She nearly always gives B what he indicates that he wants, although perhaps not invariably so. When she feels that it is best not to comply with his demands – for example, when he is too excited, over-imperious, or wants something he should not have – she is tactful in acknowledging his communication and in offering an acceptable alternative. She has "well-rounded" interactions with B, so that the transaction is smoothly completed and both she and B feel satisfied. Finally, she makes her responses temporally contingent upon B's signals arid communications.

'Insensitive' caregiving was characterised by less awareness of the child's signals; inaccuracies in interpreting them; inappropriate responses to the signals; and a lack of timeliness in these responses:

Highly insensitive: The extremely insensitive mother seems geared almost exclusively to her own wishes, moods, and activity. That is M's interventions and initiations of interaction are prompted or shaped largely by signals within herself; if they mesh with B's signals, this is often no more than coincidence. This is not to say that M never responds to B's signals; for sometimes she does if the signals are intense enough, prolonged enough, or often enough repeated. The delay in response is in itself insensitive. Furthermore, since there is usually a disparity between one's own wishes and activity and B's signals, M who is geared largely to her own signals routinely ignores or distorts the meaning of behaviour. Thus, when M responds to B's signals, her response is inappropriate in kind or fragmented and incomplete.

Using this scale, Ainsworth found that caregiver sensitivity in her Baltimore data predicted children's cooperativeness, distress, and aggression on brief everyday separations within the home and other aspects of their home behaviour. The Ainsworth sensitivity scale remained unpublished until recently, but the manuscript circulated among researchers, and the concept has been enormously influential for the subsequent study of attachment and caregiving.[4] In part, this is because, even with so many factors involved in child development, caregiver sensitivity has been found to be a notable predictor of later child outcomes. For instance, a meta-analysis by Cooke and colleagues found that insensitive caregiving was associated with child behavioural problems ($r = .14$).[5] In samples facing economic adversity, insensitive caregiving was also associated with child depression and anxiety ($r = .14$), though not in more affluent samples.

As with 'security', many have misunderstood Ainsworth's meaning regarding 'sensitivity'. This is perhaps unsurprising since in ordinary language, the term 'sensitivity', applied to caregiving, implies warmth and tenderness. As anthropologists have observed, these are qualities prised by many Western societies but are by no means important to every culture around the world.[6] However, this was not what Ainsworth intended by 'sensitivity'.

In fact, observed maternal warmth and affectionate behaviour was not associated with behaviour by children suggesting the expectation of caregiver availability in either Ainsworth's Uganda or Baltimore observations. This important finding has been supported by later attachment researchers.[7]

Ainsworth's concept of sensitivity sought to address the contingency and relevance, not the content, of interactions. More a matter of whether the caregiver and child dance well together than how many steps they take or how great the steps seem. There are important and relevant cultural and socioeconomic differences in parenting, which profoundly shape this content. However, most urban and literate parents around the world do endorse Ainsworth's concept of sensitivity as part of what they aspire to in the care they provide to infants, though there is less agreement among rural parents in nonliterate cultures both with the concept of sensitivity and with each other regarding the nature of good care.[8]

Though Ainsworth's sensitivity scale was developed for the study of infant-mother interactions, subsequent researchers have found that the construct could be readily applied with other adults and with older children without needing to be recast. It is just as relevant for considering, for instance, how a caregiver sets boundaries with their toddler or handles the emerging autonomy of their early adolescent.

The sensitivity scale was not intended to cover everything. Ainsworth herself observed other aspects of parental care that seemed important for children's expectations of access to a safe haven. As mentioned earlier, Ainsworth also developed other scales, for instance, the extent to which caregivers helped and cooperated with the child's behaviour or appeared to interfere with it. Later attachment researchers have also identified the importance of other factors contributing to children's expectations about safe haven availability, including avoidance of alarming behaviours (Chapter 4).

Later researchers have also drawn an important distinction between sensitivity to signals suggesting infant distress, and sensitivity to non-distress signals. In a study by Leerkes and colleagues, it was only the former that predicted later child socioemotional development.[9] If sensitivity was intended as an index specifically of the caregiver's availability as a safe haven by Ainsworth, the sensitivity scale is rather over-encompassing. Increasingly, attachment researchers have been interested to narrow the focus to caregiver behaviours indicating accessibility and responsiveness to the child's concerns.[10]

THE STRANGE SITUATION

In the familiar home setting, infants in Ainsworth's sample were rarely distressed, and bouts of seeking comfort from caregivers were relatively infrequent. This meant that it could take hours of observation, over several occasions, to get a reliable set of observations of an infant's typical use of their caregiver as a safe haven and secure base. Ainsworth decided to supplement her home observations with a brief, more standardised procedure that could be conducted in a simple laboratory observation room. The procedure consisted of brief episodes of toy play with the mother, interaction with a laboratory assistant, and two episodes in which the mother briefly left the observation room. Although modelled on everyday separation-reunion experiences that every infant experiences, it became known as the 'Strange Situation Procedure' (SSP) because it was conducted in an unfamiliar room.

The procedure built upon Bowlby's theory that the attachment system would be activated by separations of infants from their familiar caregivers (Chapter 1), and by encountering a novel – 'strange' – environment, also featuring an adult 'stranger'. The laboratory space also contained various toys, at a little distance from the chair for the caregiver. This was designed as a cue for the child to explore. The infant's use of the caregiver as a secure base and safe haven could therefore be observed.

The Strange Situation was not regarded by Ainsworth as an assessment of a 'thing' called attachment. Sometimes it has been discussed this way; at best this is a shorthand, but mostly it is misleading. The Strange Situation sought to mobilise the infant's expectations based on what has happened when he or she has felt anxiety in the past about the availability of the attachment figure, and allow a viewer to infer these expectations from observed behaviour.

The function of the artificial, laboratory-based procedure was to dramatise an everyday issue in the lives of infants: the question of the extent to which their experiences had led them to believe that the caregiver was available when needed. The function of the two separations and reunions was to pose this question first at a low level and then at a moderate level. The Strange Situation therefore assessed the responses of the individual infant; but this was intended, ultimately, as an indirect way of measuring differences in the history of interaction between the child and caregiver. Thus, double inferences from the child's behaviours are at stake here, that is, to expectations *and* to caregiving experiences.

Most infants responded to the Strange Situation exactly as Bowlby had anticipated. At least by the second separation they sought the availability of their caregiver, and on reunions they could be comforted and return to play. Various attachment behaviours were shown by these infants: they could crawl or waddle to their caregiver on reunion, lift their arms to be picked up, signal with a directed cry, or clamber up onto the caregiver. Closeness with the caregiver was regained when needed, a goal that could be achieved through various means.

Ainsworth's examination of her home observations revealed that the infants who exhibited distress but who could be comforted had experienced care that was relatively sensitive. The association in her data was remarkably strong: $r = .78$. She therefore labelled these infant-caregiver dyads as "secure" in the attachment relationship, since the infant's behaviour appeared to reflect confidence that the caregiver would be available when needed.

Yet some infants displayed behaviours Bowlby, Ainsworth, and colleagues had earlier described in children after their return home from hospitalisation: either i) "rejecting" and avoidant of the caregiver on reunion, or ii) "over-dependent" and "ambivalent" (Chapter 2).

The first group of children did not show more attachment behaviour as the separations and reunions progressed, and instead directed their attention and their movements away from their caregiver. These children would concentrate their attention on toys or other aspects of the room just at the moment when other infants would show distress and other attachment behaviours. Yet the quality of this attention to the toys was poor – mostly just banging them about. It seemed that the toys were being used as a distraction to avoid attending to the caregiver and other cues for the activation of the attachment system. Ainsworth ultimately came to label these infant-caregiver dyads as showing insecure "avoidant" attachment (Group A).

This avoidance was certainly not a stable trait. At home, these infants frequently showed distress and frustration with their caregivers. Ainsworth's home observations indicated that these infants had experienced relatively less sensitive care. Caregivers were also more likely to pick them up in an abrupt and interfering manner and were less likely to cuddle them. They were also more likely to show anger towards their infant. Ainsworth concluded that for avoidant infant-caregiver dyads, the attachment behavioural system was being activated by the Strange Situation, but its expression was being suppressed by the infant. Ainsworth and her student Mary Main theorised that these infants had learnt that the best way of preserving their caregiver's availability when alarmed was to avoid approaching the caregiver directly for comfort whilst maintaining a comfortable distance.

The second group seemed less able to use the caregiver as a secure base from which to explore the novel environment and were difficult to comfort on reunion with the caregiver. They also often showed frustration with the caregiver, even to the point that anger would interrupt displays of attachment behaviour. Ainsworth came to label these infant-caregiver dyads as showing insecure "resistant" attachment (Group C).

Again, these infants had generally received relatively less sensitive care according to Ainsworth's home observations. Ainsworth had the qualitative impression that the caregivers of these infants were more inconsistent in their attention to their child. This has often been repeated by later attachment researchers and phrased as a fact. However, she could not support this observation through quantitative analysis of her data and, in her final account of the classification, made no mention of inconsistent care.[11]

Rather than inconsistency, Ainsworth inferred that these infants' experiences had made them concerned about the availability of their caregiver's attention for them. This is in line with the small amount of subsequent research on specific antecedents of resistant attachment, which has found that, in situations where there are other calls on their attention, caregivers in resistant dyads are comparatively less responsive to their infants' signals than other caregivers.[12]

Subsequent attachment researchers replicated the link that Ainsworth found between sensitive caregiving and secure attachment, and between insensitive caregiving and insecure attachment. However, they have generally not found as strong an association. Ainsworth's sensitivity scale was developed on the same sample that she was studying, which likely considerably inflated the strength of the association she discovered. From a meta-analysis of 87 samples, Madigan and colleagues reported an effect size of $r = .24$.[13]

This is a moderate association. In part, this discrepancy may be due to some of the limitations with the sensitivity scale discussed earlier, and in part because of brief, relatively low-quality assessments of sensitivity in many studies. Consequently, length of sensitivity assessment was a moderating variable in the meta-analysis. The Maternal Behaviour Q-Sort, an assessment developed by Ainsworth's student David Pederson and colleagues, is based on longer periods of home observation and had an aggregated effect size of $r = .46$. Other researchers have found that repeated measurement of sensitivity leads to better prediction than one-off assessment[14] and that when a caregiver's sensitivity fluctuates over time, this may be as or more important in predicting outcomes than the average sensitivity rating.[15]

Over and above caregiver sensitivity, another influence on attachment security documented by researchers has been the emotional climate of the home, highlighting the importance of the wider caregiving context as argued in Chapter 2.[16] One illustration is inter-partner violence, which is associated with child attachment insecurity ($r = .23$).[17] This is coherent with Ainsworth's account of how the attachment system works: if a child's safe haven is itself under threat or associated with threat, this can be anticipated to hinder the child's confidence in the availability of the caregiver, irrespective of the sensitivity of one-to-one interactions between the child and that caregiver.

Other researchers have proposed that a child's temperament may play a role in the extent to which caregiver sensitivity is associated with infant attachment classifications. There are no associations between temperament and most patterns of attachment. However, temperament does seem a relevant predictor of resistant attachment ($r = .15$).[18] There may also be effects on child development of the specific combination of genetic predispositions and the care the child receives (i.e., a gene-environment interaction effect). For instance, some children may be genetically predisposed to be more vulnerable to insensitive care and/or respond more positively to sensitive care.[19]

Nonetheless, study after study has affirmed an important link between sensitive caregiving behaviours and child attachment behaviour in the Strange Situation. Intervention research with families has also shown that changes in caregiver sensitivity have predictable effects on the frequency of secure child attachment, supporting the idea of a causal relationship (see the Conclusion). For Ainsworth, in any case, it was the discovery of sensitive caregiving that was most important, and she anticipated that observations of caregiver sensitivity would have greater predictive value than a child's attachment behaviour in the Strange Situation. In fact, if it were not for the class, gender, and age differences that gave Bowlby more status than Ainsworth, it is possible that attachment theory would have been called 'sensitivity theory'. The Strange Situation is a behaviourally based measure of a child's expectations of their caregiver, inferred from child behaviour. However, observations of a caregiver's behaviour clearly offer a more direct measure of the care a child has experienced. For this reason, in principle, the Strange Situation should be validated against home observations when applied to a new population or age group, though attachment researchers have not frequently done this.

The Strange Situation was attractive for the community of developmental scientists, as a well-operationalised laboratory-based procedure. It is far more economical than extended home observations. Yet the procedure is time-consuming and difficult to learn to code. This has limited the number of people who can use the procedure and who have in depth knowledge about it as a measure. This is in stark contrast to the great public and practitioner interest in attachment theory and opens up to expectations about what attachment means that are not congruent with what the procedure actually measures. Another consequence has been that the Strange Situation has been relatively unattractive to anthropological researchers, who also tend to prefer ethnographic methods to structured observations. Looking back on the decades of research using the Strange Situation, Mesman and colleagues have observed that "the current cross-cultural database is almost absurdly small compared to the domain that should be covered."[20]

An important early study using the Strange Situation was conducted by Klaus and Karin Grossman in Bielefeld, Germany. The researchers found a much higher proportion of avoidantly attached child-caregiver dyads than the Ainsworth study. This finding fits with widespread stereotypes about Germans as a nation of emotionally suppressed individuals and has often been cited as evidence against Ainsworth. Yet subsequent German samples have found distributions much the same as those of Ainsworth, with security as the predominant pattern. Furthermore, in the Bielefeld sample, infants who received an avoidant attachment classification but who had experienced sensitive care had outcomes equivalent to those from securely attached dyads and unlike other infants from avoidantly attached dyads.[21]

Another important early cross-cultural study was conducted by Takahashi in Sapporo, Japan. The researchers found a higher proportion of resistantly attached child-caregiver dyads than the Ainsworth study. This result has frequently been used to argue that attachment theory has reduced applicability in Japan, or in Asian societies generally, due to culturally specific aspects of caregiving. However, the separations endured by the infants in the Sapporo sample were much longer than those used and recommended by Ainsworth. Therefore, it is not surprising that the infants were distressed and frustrated, contributing to a greater frequency of resistant classifications. Other Japanese samples have found distributions aligned with those of Ainsworth, with security as the predominant pattern, though there have been comparatively fewer avoidant dyads. As in other studies around the world, infant attachment classifications have been predicted by caregiver sensitivity in Japanese studies. In fact, a recent meta-analysis has reported that the association between caregiver sensitivity and Strange Situation classifications is actually strongest in Asian samples researched to date: $r = 0.40$ compared to a global aggregated effect size of $r = 0.24$.[22]

CONDITIONAL STRATEGIES

Some critics have argued that the Strange Situation represents a form of cultural imperialism or ethnocentrism: it seems implausible that three categories developed for describing a small number of middle-class Baltimore infant-mother dyads should have applicability across the globe. Yet this is a misunderstanding of Ainsworth's position. Ainsworth certainly did not assume that there were merely three 'kinds' of attachment relationships, let alone three 'kinds' of infants. Though she inadvertently gave many this impression through using categories in describing her findings, including both advocates and critics of her position. In fact, she conceptualised one universal process – the operation of safe haven/secure base dynamics through the attachment behavioural system – and alterations to its output as a result of the child's experience.

The ways that infants have available for altering the output of the attachment system is limited. Ainsworth suspected that the main two would be avoidance of the caregiver (A) or frustration with the caregiver (C). But she felt there could well be other ways of altering the output of the attachment system, especially after infancy. She had no particular investment in the distributions of avoidant and resistant classifications in different countries, except insofar as the findings could be predicted from detailed observations of caregivers' sensitivity. For Ainsworth, the only fundamental cross-cultural claim was that sensitive care would be linked to children's use of the caregiver as a secure base and safe haven. If families routinely faced a higher level of adversity within a certain culture, and if these adversities hindered the capacity of the caregiver to display the qualities of sensitive care, then a lower rate of secure attachment would be expected. Though we know of no research that has actually explicitly assessed this claim; it may or may not hold.

By contrast, Ainsworth's student Mary Main put forward a more ambitious claim. She proposed that Ainsworth's three categories of infant-caregiver attachment were a local case of a universal phenomenon for all humans. She agreed with Ainsworth that secure attachment represented the primary expression of the attachment behavioural system. She also claimed that avoidant and resistant attachment expressed opposite alterations of the output of that system. For Main, the output of a behavioural system – whether attachment, caregiving, etc. – could be minimised (attenuated) or maximised (intensified). That was the spectrum.

Main hypothesised that the basic process underpinning the difference between avoidant and resistant attachment was the direction of attention. Main theorised that any behavioural system could be minimised or maximised through direction of attention away from or towards information that would cause that system's activation. In the case of the attachment system, avoidance minimised expression of the behavioural system by the child directing attention *away* from information that might activate the attachment system. Resistant attachment kept the attachment system activated by the child keeping attention focused *towards* information that might activate the attachment system.

Main drew from ideas in evolutionary biology, including the work of Hinde (Chapter 1), in proposing the minimisation and maximisation of expressions of the attachment system as 'conditional strategies'. As usual with terminology used by attachment theorists, this phrase has a technical meaning, not apparent from the ordinary associations of the words 'conditional' and 'strategy'. With this term, Main intended to refer to a behavioural repertoire made available by human evolutionary history for solving problems of survival and/ or reproduction. Confusingly, it did not imply one way or another whether the child's behaviour was planned or beneficial to them, usual connotations of the word 'strategic'.

Main argued that avoidance and resistance represented techniques, available to humans as a result of our evolutionary history, which can be used to modify the output of the attachment system. These techniques can be anticipated to have helped infants survive in the context of more adverse circumstances, where caregivers are less able to offer sensitive care. The avoidant attachment classification represented a raised threshold for activation of the attachment system; in evolutionary perspective, it may have helped retain the availability of a caregiver who would respond negatively to a child's distress. The resistant attachment classification represented a lowered threshold for activation of the attachment system; in evolutionary perspective, it may have helped retain a caregiver's attention and activation of caregiving behaviours.

Avoidance and resistance were described as 'conditional' strategies. By this, Main meant that they are used 'on the condition' that the developmentally primary strategy (i.e., secure attachment) appears untenable: that is, a child is not able to expect direct satisfaction of the attachment system through use of the caregiver as a safe haven and secure base. She certainly did not mean to imply that secure attachment occurs without 'conditions': like Ainsworth, Main assumed that security is maintained by caregiver sensitivity and other behaviours that lead the child to continue to anticipate the availability of a safe haven and secure base.

Main anticipated that the conditional strategies would rarely be as beneficial as the primary (secure) strategy for the child in the long run, even if they could certainly have short-term advantages. This is a question currently debated by attachment researchers. Some have argued that there will be adverse environments in which avoidance or resistance are almost always likely to improve chances for survival than use of the caregiver as a safe haven and secure base. These conditional strategies may also initiate a developmental pathway that leads to distrust of the availability of others and − when faced with adversity − contribute to greater chances of successful reproduction in later life.[23]

The theory of avoidance and resistance as minimising and maximising strategies has been hugely influential. It has been a powerful framework for the design of studies and the explanation of results by

researchers and has had ready application as a model in clinical practice. Some limitations of the account should also be noted, however.

Firstly, the model has tended to freeze thinking about conditional
strategies with infancy as the ultimate and overriding model. Main
and Hesse acknowledge this problem. In their view, "development
allows humans to override a behavioural system in other ways than
the two conditional strategies, producing a wider variety of potential strategies than those available to infants".[24] However, attachment
researchers have generally failed to consider conditional strategies
after infancy and whether these are all also forms of minimising
or maximising. In general, the infant categories have instead been
imported, too often without a strong theoretical justification, to
assessments for later in the life course.

This has contributed to weaknesses in both attachment theory
and research in addressing the more varied capabilities that come
with human maturation, including our greater engagement with
cultural forms after infancy. For instance, ethologists have widely
discussed dominance as a behavioural system. But since infants do
not show such behaviour, this important feature of human life from
toddlerhood onwards has been left out of attachment theory. As a
consequence, observations of controlling behaviour shown by children towards their caregivers (Chapter 4) have lacked an ethological
framework, hindering their integration into the wider theory.

Secondly, there has been a fundamental lack of clarity among
attachment researchers and attachment-informed clinicians about
what exactly is being minimised or maximised. One consequence
has been that Main's proposal that the conditional strategies represent
minimisation and maximisation of attention to attachment-relevant
information remains insufficiently elaborated and largely untested.

What empirical work there has been has raised some questions.
For instance, Kirsh and Cassidy examined the relationship between
children's Strange Situation classifications and their recall of stories.[25]
In line with Main's attentional model, they found that avoidant
attachment was associated with poorer recall of stories where a caregiver sensitively responds to a child's requests for help. However,

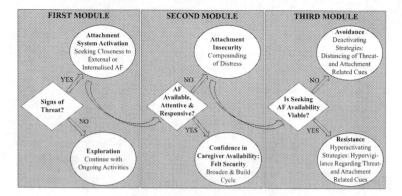

Figure 3.1 A model characterising attachment-system functioning and dynamics, and delineating hypothesised differences between secure avoidant and resistant patterns of attachment.

Source: The figure, reprinted with permission by Mario Mikulincer, is a revised and simplified version of a figure by Mikulincer and Shaver (2016)

they found that resistant attachment was associated with poorer recall of stories where a caregiver rejects the child's requests; this does not sit well with Main's prediction that resistant attachment would be associated with greater attention to potential threats to the availability of caregivers. Such findings suggest that the attentional theory of individual differences in attachment may require further elaboration and specification.

Another consequence of the lack of clarity about what exactly is being minimised or maximised has been confusion among researchers and clinicians about how to interpret one of Main's most consequential contributions to attachment theory, the disorganised attachment classification, to which we will now turn.

NOTES

1 Groh, A.M., Fearon, R.P., Bakermans-Kranenburg, M.J., van IJzendoorn, M.H., Steele, R.D., & Roisman, G.I. (2014). The significance of attachment security for children's social competence with peers: A meta-analytic study. *Attachment & Human Development*, 16(2), 103–136.

2 Pinquart, M. (2022). Associations of self-esteem with attachment to parents: A meta-analysis. *Psychological Reports*, Advance online publication.

3 Ainsworth, M., Blehar, M., Waters, E., & Wall, S. ([1978] 2015). *Patterns of Attachment: A Psychological Study of the Strange Situation*. Bristol: Psychology Press, Appendix IV.

4 Posada, G., Waters, E., Vaughn, B.E., Pederson, D.R., & Moran, G. (2021). Mary Ainsworth, ethology, and maternal sensitivity. In E. Waters, B. Vaughn, & H. Waters (Eds.), *Measuring Attachment: Developmental Assessment Across the Lifespan* (pp. 1–36). New York: Guilford.

5 Cooke, J.E., Deneault, A.A., Devereux, C., Eirich, R., Fearon, R.P., & Madigan, S. (2022). Parental sensitivity and child behavioral problems: A meta-analytic review. *Child Development*, 93(5), 1231–1248.

6 LeVine, R.A. (2004). Challenging expert knowledge: Findings from an African study of infant care and development. In U.P. Gielen & J.L. Roopnarine (Eds.), *Childhood and Adolescence: Cross-Cultural Perspectives and Applications* (pp. 149–165). Westport, CT: Greenwood Publishing.

7 Bailey, H.N., Bernier, A., Bouvette-Turcot, A.A., Tarabulsy, G.M., Pederson, D.R., & Becker-Stoll, F. (2017). Deconstructing maternal sensitivity: Predictive relations to mother-child attachment in home and laboratory settings. *Social Development*, 26(4), 679–693.

8 Mesman, J., Van IJzendoorn, M., Behrens, K., Carbonell, O.A., Cárcamo, R., Cohen-Paraira, I., . . . Kondo-Ikemura, K. (2016). Is the ideal mother a sensitive mother? Beliefs about early childhood parenting in mothers across the globe. *International Journal of Behavioral Development*, 40(5), 385–397.

9 Leerkes, E.M., & Zhou, N. (2018). Maternal sensitivity to distress and attachment outcomes: Interactions with sensitivity to nondistress and infant temperament. *Journal of Family Psychology*, 32(6), 753–761.

10 Woodhouse, S.S., Scott, J.R., Hepworth, A.D., & Cassidy, J. (2020). Secure base provision: A new approach to examining links between maternal caregiving and infant attachment. *Child Development*, 91(1), 249–265.

11 Ainsworth, M.D.S., & Eichberg, C.G. (1991). Effects on infant-mother attachment of mother's experience related to loss of an attachment figure. In C.M. Parkes, J. Stevenson-Hinde, & P. Marris (Eds.), *Attachment Across the Life Cycle* (pp. 160–183). London: Routledge, p. 162.

12 Vondra, J.I., Shaw, D.S., & Kevenides, M.C. (1995). Predicting infant attachment classification from multiple, contemporaneous measures of

maternal care. *Infant Behavior and Development*, 18(4), 415–425; Harel, J., & Scher, A. (2003). Insufficient responsiveness in ambivalent mother–infant relationships. *Infant Behavior and Development*, 26(3), 371–383.

13 Madigan, S., Deneault, A.-A., Duschinsky, R., Bakermans-Kranenburg, M.J., Schuengel, C., van IJzendoorn, M.H., Ly, A., Fearon, P.R.M., Eirich, R., & Verhage, M.L. (in press). Parent sensitivity and child attachment: A meta-analysis revisited. *Psychological Bulletin*.

14 Lindhiem, O., Bernard, K., & Dozier, M. (2011). Maternal sensitivity: Within-person variability and the utility of multiple assessments. *Child Maltreatment*, 16(1), 41–50.

15 Eller, J., Magro, S.W., Roisman, G.I., & Simpson, J.A. (2022). The predictive significance of fluctuations in early maternal sensitivity for secure base script knowledge and relationship effectiveness in adulthood. *Journal of Social and Personal Relationships*, 39(10), 3044–3058.

16 Raikes, H.A., & Thompson, R.A. (2005). Links between risk and attachment security: Models of influence. *Journal of Applied Developmental Psychology*, 26(4), 440–455.

17 McIntosh, J.E., Tan, E.S., Levendosky, A.A., & Holtzworth-Munroe, A. (2021). Mothers' experience of intimate partner violence and subsequent offspring attachment security ages 1–5 years: A meta-analysis. *Trauma, Violence, & Abuse*, 22(4), 885–899.

18 Groh, A.M., Narayan, A.J., Bakermans-Kranenburg, M.J., Roisman, G.I., Vaughn, B.E., Fearon, R.P., & van IJzendoorn, M.H. (2017). Attachment and temperament in the early life course: A meta-analytic review. *Child Development*, 88(3), 770–795.

19 Van IJzendoorn, M.H., & Bakermans-Kranenburg, M.J. (2012). Integrating temperament and attachment. The differential susceptibility paradigm. In M. Zentner & R.L. Shiner (Eds.), *Handbook of Temperament* (pp. 403–424). New York: Guilford.

20 Mesman, J., van IJzendoorn, M.H., & Sagi-Schwartz, S. (2016). Cross-cultural patterns of attachment: Universal and contextual dimensions. In J. Cassidy & P. Shaver (Eds.), *Handbook of Attachment*, 3rd ed. (pp. 790–815). New York: Guilford, p. 809.

21 Grossmann, K.E., Grossmann, K., & Schwan, A. (1986). Capturing the wider view of attachment: A reanalysis of Ainsworth's strange situation. In C.E. Izard & P.B. Read (Eds.), *Measuring Emotions in Infants and Children*, vol. 2 (pp. 124–171). Cambridge: Cambridge University Press.

22 Madigan, S., Deneault, A.-A., Duschinsky, R., Bakermans-Kranenburg, M.J., Schuengel, C., van IJzendoorn, M.H., Ly, A., Fearon, P.R.M., Eirich, R., & Verhage, M.L. (in press). Parent sensitivity and child attachment: A meta-analysis revisited. *Psychological Bulletin*.

23 Belsky, J., Houts, R.M., & Fearon, R.P. (2010). Infant attachment security and the timing of puberty: Testing an evolutionary hypothesis. *Psychological Science*, 21(9), 1195–1201.

24 Mary Main and Erik Hesse, personal communication, August 2019.

25 Kirsh, S.J., & Cassidy, J. (1997). Preschoolers' attention to and memory for attachment-relevant information. *Child Development*, 68(6), 1143–1153.

FURTHER RECOMMENDED READING

Duschinsky, R. (2020). Mary Ainsworth and the strange situation procedure. In *Cornerstones of Attachment Research*. Oxford: Oxford University Press.

Mesman, J., van IJzendoorn, M.H., & Sagi-Schwartz, S. (2016). Cross-cultural patterns of attachment: Universal and contextual dimensions. In J. Cassidy & P. Shaver (Eds.), *Handbook of Attachment*, 3rd ed. (pp. 790–815). New York: Guilford.

Simpson, J.A., & Belsky, J. (2016). Attachment theory within a modern evolutionary framework. In J. Cassidy & P. Shaver (Eds.), *Handbook of Attachment*, 3rd ed. (pp. 91–116). New York: Guilford.

Mikulincer, M. & Shaver, P. (2017) A Model of Attachment-System Functioning and Dynamics in Adulthood. In M. Mikulincer and P. R. Shaver (Eds.), *Attachment in adulthood: Structure, dynamics, and change* (pp. 27 – 46). The Guilford Press.

4

DISORGANISED ATTACHMENT AND ATTACHMENT BEYOND THE EARLY YEARS

DISORGANISED ATTACHMENT

As we saw in Chapter 1, Bowlby and his collaborator Hinde came to conceptualise attachment as a 'behavioural system': a disposition, primed by evolution, to respond to the environment in such a way as to achieve a particular goal, drawing in part on learnt experience and in part on certain behaviours disposed by the evolution of the species. They also described other behavioural systems, such as the disposition to explore new environments; the disposition to flee from sources of alarm; the disposition to affiliate with others; the disposition to display aggression when frustrated; and the disposition to provide care to offspring.

In his observations of animal behaviour in the 1960s, Hinde saw that these behavioural systems could come into conflict. For instance, in his detailed study of the behaviour of chaffinches, he found that when the bird encountered something strange or novel, two behavioural systems would be activated: both the disposition to explore and the disposition to escape. Where cues favoured the activation of one behavioural system, it tended to dominate, but with the other still present to a degree. For instance, the bird might

DOI: 10.4324/9781003020349-5

approach to explore, but cautiously and with wings set for a rapid exit if needed.

In other circumstances, where cues were about equal, Hinde observed 'conflict behaviour' such as the quick transition between one tendency and the other, poorly coordinated combinations, freezing in place, misdirected movements, or signs of confusion or tension. Hinde also observed conflict behaviour shown by baby birds towards their parents. For example, if the parent bird made a sudden approach, the infants could be observed to seek their parent, but also to show indications of a disposition to flee or other forms of conflict behaviour.

Bowlby was absolutely fascinated by Hinde's observations, and he saw forms of conflict behaviour in ordinary human life. If Bowlby felt two conflicting inclinations – to pick up the telephone, and to finish his cup of tea – he might find himself attempting to do both in an uncoordinated way, freeze in place for a moment, or scratch his head. Yet Bowlby also saw more sustained and intrusive forms of conflict behaviour in mental health symptoms. He considered that some of the displays of behavioural conflict or confusion among World War II veterans, who he treated in his work as a war psychiatrist, may have stemmed from a prolonged and intense conflict between fear and duty.

Hinde's concept of conflict behaviours also interested Mary Main, who conducted one of the first studies using the Strange Situation procedure after Ainsworth's original work. Now that she was looking out for them, Main documented various forms of conflict behaviour by the infants toward their parents. These included "stereotypies; hand-flapping; echolalia; inappropriate affect (inexplicable fears, inappropriate laughter) and other behaviours appearing out of context".[1]

In some cases, the child's use of the caregiver as a safe haven seemed only briefly interrupted by these behaviours. In other cases, they dominated the child's response on reunion, making it difficult to fit the case into one of Ainsworth's three categories. Ainsworth advised that the cases should be 'force-classified' into one of her three categories. However, she continued to regard conflict behaviour as important: the final pages of *Patterns of Attachment* were dedicated to urging subsequent researchers to consider the meaning of conflict behaviours seen in the Strange Situation, and their different potential causes.

As we saw in the previous chapter, Main came to the dramatic conclusion that the three patterns of infant response observed by Ainsworth in the Strange Situation represented the three basic repertoires for managing the output of *any* behavioural system. The behavioural system could be expressed directly, or, through a conditional strategy, the behavioural system could be minimised or maximised through direction of attention away from or towards information that would cause its activation. Interruptions or exceptions to the Ainsworth patterns were therefore even more salient for Main than they were for Ainsworth, since they were potentially revealing something fundamental about the nature of attachment.

After finishing her doctorate, Main took up a post at University of California, Berkeley. Main's research group began collecting Strange Situations with mothers and fathers, initiating a longitudinal study. Together with her graduate student Judith Solomon, Main began to review conflict behaviours shown by this sample, as well as tapes sent to them of conflict behaviour shown by infants from other samples. Most of the conflict behaviour they saw was much the same as that described by Hinde, including sequential or simultaneous displays of contradictory behaviour; undirected, misdirected, or incomplete movements; stereotypies, mistimed movements and anomalous postures; and freezing or stilling; and signs of confusion.

Main and Solomon also observed some displays of apprehension of the caregiver, especially by infants from the tapes sent over from colleagues conducting research with high-risk or maltreating families. These were not technically conflict behaviour since the child's apprehension could be coherently expressed. However, Main and Solomon decided that apprehension of the caregiver should be treated as a kind of conflict because it was contrary to the attachment system. They therefore put displays of apprehension together with conflict behaviour into an overarching category, which they termed 'disorganised attachment', and proposed this as an additional insecure classification for the Strange Situation.

In a recent meta-analysis of 285 studies and over 20,000 parent-child dyads, Madigan and colleagues found that the global distribution of infant-parent attachment was 51.6% secure, 14.7% avoidant, 10.2% resistant, and 23.5% disorganised.[2] Yet among these studies, it still remains to be investigated whether a child's display of conflict, confusion, and apprehension towards a caregiver have the same meaning. The form of the coding system created by Main and Solomon has made this question difficult to pursue empirically. Researchers have instead examined associations between the disorganised classification as a whole and other phenomena, in particular caregiving precursors and developmental outcomes.

Groh and colleagues reported from a meta-analysis of 42 studies that there is no link between disorganised attachment and later anxiety or depression.[3] However, Fearon and colleagues reported a meta-analysis of 69 studies, documenting associations with attentional and behavioural problems for avoidant ($r = .06$) and disorganised attachment ($r = .17$).[4] The association was stronger in samples with a parent with mental health difficulties ($r = .23$). It was much stronger when child behaviour was assessed by an observer ($r = .29$) rather than reported by the child's mother ($r = .11$). It may be that the social and psychological processes disrupting the attachment relationship may also hinder the caregiver's capacity to accurately identify or to report on their experiences in attachment relationships (Chapter 5). In another meta-analysis, researchers have also documented other associations of disorganised attachment, including associations with poorer social competence and friendships ($r = .12$).[5] Though there is some evidence for links between disorganised attachment and dissociative problems, a recent study found no association between disorganised attachment and later psychotic symptoms, contrary to the expectations of some attachment theorists.[6]

Overall, disorganised attachment is clearly a relevant classification for understanding child development. However attachment

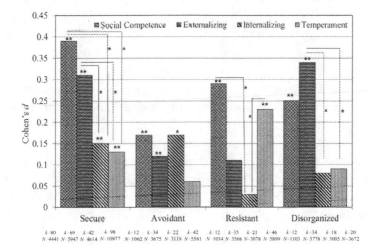

Figure 4.1 Combined meta-analytical effect sizes for the four attachment
categories, concerning social competence, externalising and
internalising behaviour problems, and temperament. Each category is contrasted against all other categories combined. For
instance, Secure = Secure vs. all insecure categories combined,
and Disorganised = Disorganised vs. all other patterns combined.
Asterisks over bars indicate significant combined effects sizes for
contrasts with other categories. For instance, secure attachment
was meta-analytically associated with higher levels of social competence, and lower levels of internalising and externalising behaviour problems. Asterisks along lines represent significant differences
in effects sizes for a certain category. For instance, the effect size
for social competence, for children classified as secure, was significantly stronger than the effect size for internalising problems.

Source: The figure is reprinted, with permission, from Groh et al. (2017)

researchers agree that associations with adverse developmental outcomes are not sufficiently strong for disorganised attachment to be
taken as an indication of pathology in itself.[7]

ALARMING CAREGIVER BEHAVIOUR

Researchers have been interested to understand factors that predict
children showing conflict, confusion, or apprehension towards their

caregivers in the Strange Situation. In community samples, around 20% of infants show a sufficient degree of such behaviour, as measured by the strange situation procedure, for a primary disorganised classification to be given. However, in samples of young children who have been maltreated, and in samples from families facing multiple adversities, a slight majority receive a disorganised classification.

Main's collaborator and husband, Erik Hesse, developed the idea that the conflicted, confused, and apprehensive behaviours that Main and Solomon were seeing in the Strange Situation might be caused by the child's experiences of alarming behaviour by their caregiver. When distressed, a child will want to seek the caregiver as a safe haven (Chapter 1). They will direct their attention towards the caregiver and show attachment behaviour. In the case of resistant attachment, they will keep attention locked on the caregiver, even when they are physically available. In the case of avoidant attachment, they will keep attention directed to the environment, playing with toys near the caregiver but not seeking direct contact.

But Hesse asked: what if the caregiver's behaviour were itself alarming? Then the child's attention would be drawn to the caregiver (as a source of anticipated safety), but the child would also be motivated to avoid or flee from the caregiver (as a source of anticipated danger). He proposed that this would result in a positive feedback loop, forming a pathway to conflicted, confused, or apprehensive behaviour by the child towards their caregiver when the child is distressed, as in the Strange Situation.

Based on analysis of observations of infant–caregiver interaction in their Berkeley study, Hesse and Main created a system for coding observations of alarming caregiver behaviours. This included behaviours that might frighten the child, such as threats, but also other behaviours that Hesse and Main inferred might evoke alarm about the caregiver's availability as a safe haven, such as a period of zoning out/dissociation by the parent.

It was anticipated by Hesse and Main that alarming behaviour might be shown not just by maltreating parents but also by those who were suffering from unresolved loss or trauma. Subsequent researchers have added that alarming caregiver behaviours may be expected where a parent feels overwhelmed and helpless in the face of their current circumstances.[8]

For instance, meta-analytic research on studies using the strange situation has indicated socioeconomic stressors as one such context: disorganised attachment is more common in samples facing socioeconomic stress than in other contexts (31.3% vs. 20.6%).[9] In fact, in samples facing the ramifications of five socioeconomic risks, where feelings of concern and helplessness may be especially pervasive, disorganised attachment is common. Rates are as high as for samples known to social services for child maltreatment ($r = .51$).[10]

Madigan and colleagues conducted a meta-analysis of studies that had used the Hesse and Main coding system in observing parents and their children in free play and separately in the Strange Situation. They found that in cases where alarming parental behaviours were observed, child-parent attachments were 3.7 times more likely to be classified as disorganised ($r = .34$).[11] This suggests alarming caregiver behaviour is indeed, as Hesse predicted, an important pathway to disorganised attachment, albeit not the whole story.

An elaboration of the Hesse and Main system was subsequently developed by Lyons-Ruth and colleagues. This coding system (AMBIANCE) assesses five dimensions of 'disrupted parental communication' with the child: negative-intrusive behaviour; role confusion; disorientation; affective communication errors; and withdrawal from the child. Some of these dimensions overlap to an extent with Hesse and Main's system. Whereas the Hesse and Main system has only been available to a limited group of researchers, training is available annually in AMBIANCE, and efforts are currently underway to evaluate a brief version of AMBIANCE for use in routine clinical practice.[12] This represents an exciting and potentially promising development for bridging the research-practice divide, though more empirical work is needed.

It is also important to note that disorganised attachment is something quite different from an 'attachment disorder', which is a technical term in psychiatry for when a child shows no attachment behaviours to their familiar caregivers (i.e., reactive attachment disorder). 'Attachment disorder' has been a concern among psychiatrists, but there has been relatively little empirical research, in part because it is quite rare, and in part because until recently there were few scientifically validated tools for assessing the condition.[13] There is only minimal overlap between children who show conflict, confusion, and apprehension to their caregiver in the Strange Situation and reactive attachment disorder. This is understandable following the reasoning of Main and Hesse: a child must first be attached for conflict behaviours as regards approaching or avoiding the caregiver to arise. Disorganised attachment is regarded as a marker of vulnerability for later development, not a clinical disorder.

DEVELOPMENT AND CHANGE

In the 1960s, Bowlby introduced the term 'internal working models' to convey the importance of mental representations of actual experiences, particularly in attachment relationships. In later life, he dropped the term 'internal working model', tending to just write more simply and clearly about the *expectations* we hold about attachment figures. Bowlby theorised that expectations about the availability of others as a safe haven and/or secure base would be relatively stable over time, for several reasons: our environment may well remain stable; our expectations may lead us to behave in ways that make them self-fulfilling; and it is difficult to change our expectations deliberately even if we want to. Nonetheless, he was also certain that our expectations can and do change, if sometimes rather slowly, for instance, in response to changes in our relationships.

Main and her collaborator Jude Cassidy were interested to examine how expectations about the availability of caregivers might be expressed in the behaviour of older children. They invited families who had participated in Main's Strange Situation studies to come back to the laboratory 5 years later, and conducted an extended Strange Situation in which the caregiver was away for an hour. The parent-child relationship was classified as secure if on reunion they seemed calm and relaxed and happy to communicate with their parent. The relationship was classified as avoidant if the child responded only minimally on reunion, directing attention to the toys in the room rather than the parent's greeting. The relationship was classified as resistant if the child seemed focused on maximising the caregiver's availability or relatedness, for instance, jumping up on to the parent's lap. Unlike in infancy, resistant attachment was not coded on the basis of displays of frustration with the caregiver for being away, as this was seen by Main and Cassidy to be less expectable by age 6.

Main and Cassidy characterised the relationships as disorganised if the child's behaviour towards the caregiver seemed conflicted, confused, or apprehensive – as in infancy – or else focused on controlling the parent. 'Controlling-punitive' behaviour was coded if the child seemed to be ordering the parent about on reunion – "Sit down and shut up, and keep your eyes closed! I said, keep them closed!"– or stonewalling them. 'Controlling-caregiving' behaviour was coded if the child appeared to be attempting to look after their parent on reunion. For instance, one child asked: "Are you tired, Mommy? Would you like to sit down and I'll bring you some [pretend] tea?"[14] Main and Cassidy theorised that in controlling-punitive behaviour, the anger behavioural system was being used to direct the caregiver and ensure they remained, to an extent, available as a safe haven. In the case of controlling-caregiving behaviour, the caregiving behavioural system was serving this role.

Controlling-punitive and controlling-caregiving behaviour may be additional 'conditional strategies': behavioural repertoires made available by human evolutionary history that make survival more likely when conditions do not reward use of a more direct strategy. Main and Hesse have admitted they are not sure.[15]

Around twice as many children show conflicted, confused, or apprehensive behaviour (64%) as a controlling strategy (36%) across both preschool and middle childhood.[16] In general, conflicted, confused, or apprehensive behaviour is associated with the least positive outcomes across a range of domains.[17] The controlling-punitive subtype is associated with more behavioural difficulties. By contrast, there is only sparce evidence that controlling-caregiving behaviour is associated with poor later development.

After Main and Cassidy's pioneering work, other observation-based coding systems have been developed for coding attachment classifications after infancy. These include the Marvin-Cassidy Preschool Attachment Classification System, Crittenden's Preschool Assessment of Attachment, the Manchester Child Attachment Story Task, and Brumariu's Middle Childhood Attachment Strategies coding system. These have all been based to a greater or lesser extent on aspects of the Ainsworth Strange Situation and the Main and Cassidy 6-year system.

An exception is the Attachment Q-Sort (AQS), which is a well-validated method that can be used by researchers to code observations of infants or older children in normal interactions. Though the Strange Situation remains the dominant measure, about a fifth of all attachment research with children uses the AQS, with growing use over time. Whereas the Strange Situation uses separations and reunions to sharply bring out children's expectations about their caregiver's availability in times of need, the AQS focuses more directly on observing what children seem to be expecting from their caregiver in ordinary settings. This may be one reason that associations are stronger between separate observations of caregiver sensitivity (measured with the Ainsworth scale) and the AQS ($r = .31$) than for the Strange Situation ($r = .24$).[18] The AQS was originally coded just for security-insecurity rather than different forms of insecurity. Though, even with this measure, a version with the familiar four categories has subsequently been introduced.[19]

Attachment researchers have been interested in whether, as Bowlby predicted, expectations about safe haven and secure base availability would be partially stable over time. A first attempt to study this was by Waters, who conducted the Strange Situation in the 1970s with 50 middle-class parent-child dyads at 12 months and 18 months. Forty-eight out of the 50 relationships received the same Strange Situation classification at the two timepoints.[20] This finding was taken at the time to indicate that expectations about caregivers were exceptionally stable, perhaps even rather impervious to change in the short term. Sometimes Bowlby had implied this, especially in his early popular writings, and Waters' results seemed to be confirmation.

However, Waters also worked with colleagues on a second study, with 100 parent–child dyads living in poverty. In this second study, only 62 received the same classification at 18 months. Nonetheless the changes were often expectable according to attachment theory. So, for instance, relationships that changed from secure at 12 months to insecure at 18 months were generally those where the parent had experienced more hardship in the meantime, which could be anticipated to have hindered their capacity to notice and respond to their child's signals.[21]

Many subsequent studies have been conducted looking at the stability of attachment classifications over time. A meta-analysis by Opie of 79 studies found notable, if moderate, evidence of stability over time ($r = 0.28$).[22] An interesting finding was that security is more stable than resistant or disorganised insecure attachment classifications. This suggests that a child is more likely to keep hold of a sense of their caregiver's availability, even in the face of changing circumstances, than they are to keep hold of a sense of their caregiver's unavailability as a safe haven and secure base. It may be that, like a lot of skills, once we learn to use an attachment figure as a secure base, we do not then forget it. It could also be that, as children get older, they are more able to signal and draw availability from a stressed or distracted parent.

Yet caregiver behaviour, which predicts attachment classifications, is also relatively stable over time. For instance, Behrens and colleagues assessed caregiver sensitivity at 12 months and 3.5 years in two different contexts, finding extensive continuity ($r = .42$).[23] Caregiver sensitivity also predicts children's externalising difficulties ($r = .14$) equally well as the Strange Situation ($r = .15$).[24] The question therefore arises as to whether the apparent stability and effects of attachment are, in fact, entirely or partially an effect of the stability of care the child receives, such as the stability of insensitive or alarming caregiving behaviour over time.

The first study to address the matter empirically was conducted by Beijersbergen and colleagues in 2012. Maternal sensitivity and infant attachment were assessed at 1 year of age among children who had been adopted early in infancy. When these research participants were 14 years old, maternal sensitivity was assessed by asking the adolescent and their parent to discuss a difficult topic in their relationship. The adolescents were also interviewed to examine their expectations about attachment relationships using the Adult Attachment Interview (Chapter 5).

Beijersbergen and colleagues found no continuity at all between expectations about attachment relationships displayed by infants in the Strange Situation and the expectations manifest in their accounts of their lives in the Adult Attachment Interview. However, maternal sensitivity at age 1 and age 14 predicted continuity of secure attachment, seen as expectations about the availability of attachment figures as a safe haven and secure base. And when children received insensitive care at 1 year of age, but caregiver sensitivity was seen in the discussion at 14 years old, this predicted a change in attachment pattern from insecure to secure. The researchers concluded that continuity of attachment pattern appears to be very much dependent on continuity of the kind of caregiving the child receives. They argued that, going forward, "attachment theory should be a theory of sensitive parenting as much as it is a theory of attachment."[25]

In terms of the relative importance of measurement of caregiver sensitivity vs. the Strange Situation, the available research suggests that the former may be more important. A study by Belsky and Fearon of 1,053 children and parents over time found that insecurely attached children who subsequently experienced sensitive parenting had considerably better later outcomes than secure children who subsequently experienced less sensitive parenting. The same result held across a range of outcomes including child behavioural difficulties, social competence, and language skills.[26]

Such findings suggest that both general caregiver sensitivity and children's specific expectations about caregiver availability are relevant for child development. Nonetheless, over time, attachment researchers have come to give greater priority to measures of sensitivity and alarming caregiver behaviour, perhaps now surpassing the importance assigned to the Strange Situation. In part, this may be a result of the very positive findings from trials of interventions focused on supporting caregiver sensitivity (see Chapter 7). In a recent consensus statement, it was recommended by attachment researchers that practitioners give greater priority to measurement of caregiver behaviour rather than child attachment when looking to understand the dynamics of a family and judge whether or how to pursue an intervention.[27]

NOTES

1 Main, M. (1977). Analysis of a peculiar form of reunion behavior seen in some daycare children: Its history and sequelae in children who are home-reared. In R. Webb (Ed.), *Social Development in Childhood* (pp. 33–78). Baltimore: The John Hopkins University Press, p. 70.

2 Madigan, S., Fearon, R.M.P., van IJzendoorn, M.H., Duschinsky, R., Schuengel, C., Bakermans-Kranenburg, M.J., Ly, A., Cooke, J.E., Deneault, A.-A., Oosterman, M., & Verhage, M.L. (in press). The first 20,000 strange situation procedures: A meta-analytic review. *Psychological Bulletin*.

3 Groh, A.M., Roisman, G.I., van IJzendoorn, M.H., Bakermans-Kranenburg, M.J., & Fearon, R.P. (2012). The significance of insecure and disorganized attachment for children's internalizing symptoms: A meta-analytic study. *Child Development*, 83(2), 591–610.

4 Fearon, R.P., Bakermans-Kranenburg, M.J., van IJzendoorn, M.H., Lapsley, A.M., & Roisman, G.I. (2010). The significance of insecure attachment and disorganization in the development of children's externalizing behavior: A meta-analytic study. *Child Development*, 81(2), 435–456.

5 Groh, A.M., Fearon, R.P., Bakermans-Kranenburg, M.J., Van IJzendoorn, M.H., Steele, R.D., & Roisman, G.I. (2014). The significance of attachment security for children's social competence with peers: A meta-analytic study. *Attachment & Human Development*, 16(2), 103–136.

6 Hidalgo, A.C., Steenkamp, L., Bolhuis, K., Tiemeier, H., Bakermans-Kranenburg, M., & van IJzendoorn, M.H. (2022). P505. Infant-parent attachment and psychotic symptoms: The neurodevelopmental origins of psychosis. *Biological Psychiatry*, 91(9), S292–S293.

7 Granqvist, P., Sroufe, L.A., Dozier, M., Hesse, E., Steele, M., van IJzendoorn, M., . . . Duschinsky, R. (2017). Disorganized attachment in infancy: A review of the phenomenon and its implications for clinicians and policy-makers. *Attachment & Human Development*, 19(6), 534–558.

8 George, C., & Solomon, J. (Eds.). (2011). *Disorganized Attachment and Caregiving*. New York: Guilford.

9 Madigan, S., Fearon, R.M.P., van IJzendoorn, M.H., Duschinsky, R., Schuengel, C., Bakermans-Kranenburg, M.J., Ly, A., Cooke, J.E., Deneault, A.-A., Oosterman, M., & Verhage, M.L. (in press). The first 20,000 strange situation procedures: A meta-analytic review. *Psychological Bulletin*.

10 Cyr, C., Euser, E.M., Bakermans-Kranenburg, M.J., & Van IJzendoorn, M.H. (2010). Attachment security and disorganization in maltreating and high-risk families: A series of meta-analyses. *Development & Psychopathology*, 22(1), 87–108.

11 Madigan, S., Bakermans-Kranenburg, M.J., Van IJzendoorn, M.H., Moran, G., Pederson, D.R., & Benoit, D. (2006). Unresolved states of mind, anomalous parental behavior, and disorganized attachment: A review and meta-analysis of a transmission gap. *Attachment & Human Development*, 8(2), 89–111.

12 Madigan, S., Eirich, R., Racine, N., Borland-Kerr, C., Cooke, J.E., Devereux, C., . . . Lyons-Ruth, K. (2021). Feasibility of training service providers on the AMBIANCE-Brief measure for use in community settings. *Infant Mental Health Journal*, 42(3), 438–451.

13 Monette, S., Cyr, C., Terradas, M.M., Couture, S., Minnis, H., & Lehmann, S. (2022). Development and validation of a measure of attachment disorders based on DSM-5 criteria: The Early TRAuma-Related Disorders Questionnaire (ETRADQ). *Assessment*, 29(3), 556–571.

14 Hesse, E., & Main, M. (2000). Disorganized infant, child, and adult attachment: Collapse in behavioral and attentional strategies. *Journal of the American Psychoanalytic Association*, 48(4), 1097–1127, pp. 1106–1107.

15 Mary Main and Erik Hesse, personal communication, August 2019.

16 Deneault, A.-A., et al. (2023). A meta-analysis of the distribution of preschool and early childhood attachment as assessed in the strange situation procedure and its modified versions. *Attachment & Human Development*, 25(2), 322–351.

17 O'connor, E., Bureau, J.F., Mccartney, K., & Lyons-Ruth, K. (2011). Risks and outcomes associated with disorganized/controlling patterns of attachment at age three years in the national institute of child health & human development study of early child care and youth development. *Infant Mental Health Journal*, 32(4), 450–472.

18 Madigan, S., Deneault, A.-A., Duschinsky, R., Bakermans-Kranenburg, M.J., Schuengel, C., van IJzendoorn, M.H., Ly, A., Fearon, P.R.M., Eirich, R., & Verhage, M.L. (in press). Parent sensitivity and child attachment: A meta-analysis revisited. *Psychological Bulletin*.

19 Kirkland, J., Bimler, D., Drawneek, A., McKim, M., & Schölmerich, A. (2004). An alternative approach for the analyses and interpretation of attachment sort items. *Early Child Development and Care*, 174(7–8), 701–719.

20 Waters, E. (1978). The reliability and stability of individual differences in infant–mother attachment. *Child Development*, 49(2), 483–494.

21 Vaughn, B., Egeland, B., Sroufe, L.A., & Waters, E. (1979). Individual differences in infant–mother attachment at twelve and eighteen months: Stability and change in families under stress. *Child Development*, 971–975.

22 Opie, J.E., McIntosh, J.E., Esler, T.B., Duschinsky, R., George, C., Schore, A., . . . Olsson, C.A. (2021). Early childhood attachment stability and change: A meta-analysis. *Attachment & Human Development*, 23(6), 897–930.

23 Behrens, K.Y., Parker, A.C., & Kulkofsky, S. (2014). Stability of maternal sensitivity across time and contexts with Q-sort measures. *Infant and Child Development*, 23(5), 532–541.

24 Fearon, R.P., Bakermans-Kranenburg, M.J., Van IJzendoorn, M.H., Lapsley, A.M., & Roisman, G.I. (2010). The significance of insecure attachment and disorganization in the development of children's externalizing behavior: A meta-analytic study. *Child Development*, 81(2), 435–456; Cooke, J.E., Deneault, A.A., Devereux, C., Eirich, R., Fearon, R.P., & Madigan, S. (2022). Parental sensitivity and child behavioral problems: A meta-analytic review. *Child Development*, 93(5), 1231–1248.

25 Beijersbergen, M.D., Juffer, F., Bakermans-Kranenburg, M.J., & van IJzendoorn, M.H. (2012). Remaining or becoming secure: Parental sensitive support predicts attachment continuity from infancy to adolescence in a longitudinal adoption study. *Developmental Psychology*, 48(5), 1277–1282, p. 1281.

26 Belsky, J., & Fearon, R.P. (2002). Early attachment security, subsequent maternal sensitivity, and later child development: Does continuity in development depend upon continuity of caregiving? *Attachment & Human Development*, 4(3), 361–387.

27 Forslund, T., Granqvist, P., van IJzendoorn, M.H., Sagi-Schwartz, A., Glaser, D., Steele, M., . . . Duschinsky, R. (2022). Attachment goes to court: Child protection and custody issues. *Attachment & Human Development*, 24(1), 1–52.

FURTHER RECOMMENDED READING

Granqvist, P., Sroufe, L.A., Dozier, M., Hesse, E., Steele, M., van IJzendoorn, M., . . . Duschinsky, R. (2017). Disorganized attachment in infancy: A review of the phenomenon and its implications for clinicians and policy-makers. *Attachment & Human Development*, 19(6), 534–558.

Groh, A.M., Fearon, R.P., van IJzendoorn, M.H., Bakermans-Kranenburg, M.J., & Roisman, G.I. (2017). Attachment in the early life course: Meta-analytic evidence for its role in socioemotional development. *Child Development Perspectives*, 11(1), 70–76.

Waters, E., Vaughn, B.E., & Waters, H.S. (2021). *Measuring Attachment: Developmental Assessment Across the Lifespan*. New York: Guilford Press.

5

THE ADULT ATTACHMENT INTERVIEW AND ATTACHMENT IN ADOLESCENCE

Although attachment theory initially focused on social interactions and the growth of security in infancy, one of its greatest strengths is its relevance across the lifespan. Infant attachment is primarily conceptualised in terms of the child's expectations about the availability of a safe haven and secure base provided by their familiar caregivers. However, with cognitive and emotional development, relationships are less a matter of recent experience and increasingly involve building mental models based on a longer history of interactions with attachment figures. We use these mental models to organise our own behaviour towards attachment figures, especially parents and close relationship partners. Mental models may also come into play when we find ourselves, as parents, providing rather than seeking a safe haven and secure base for children.

Some attachment researchers have conducted direct observational research on secure base and safe haven behaviour after childhood.[1] In general, attachment researchers have focused on the stories we construct about our experiences. In particular, researchers have been concerned with how adults and adolescents process attachment-relevant information by looking at autobiographical narratives. This focus follows the work of Mary Main and colleagues at Berkeley,

DOI: 10.4324/9781003020349-6

who developed the Adult Attachment Interview. In this chapter, we first describe the Adult Attachment Interview, its development, and its classifications and correlates. In a second section, we focus specifically on one of its key classifications, unresolved/disorganised states of mind for loss or abuse. The third and final section examines adolescence as a transitional period for attachment processes.

THE ADULT ATTACHMENT INTERVIEW

As we saw in the previous chapter, Main and colleagues recalled participants to the laboratory five years after they had been originally seen in the Strange Situation. Separations and reunions were conducted, with mothers and fathers out of the room for an hour. During these separations, the two parents were interviewed individually about their own experiences growing up and their perspective now on their caregivers. Main and colleagues called this interview the "Adult Attachment Interview" (AAI) since the questions focused on participants' experiences in attachment relationships, including specific questions around any experiences of major separations or rejection or threatening behaviour by caregivers.

OPENING QUESTIONS OF THE AAI:

1. Could you start by helping me get oriented to your early family situation, and where you lived and so on? If you could tell me where you were born, whether you moved around much, what your family did at various times for a living?

2. I'd like you to try to describe your relationship with your parents as a young child if you could start from as far back as you can remember?

3. Now I'd like to ask you to choose five adjectives or words that reflect your relationship with your mother starting from as far back as you can remember in early childhood – as early as you can go, but say, age 5 to 12 is fine. I know this may take a bit of time, so go ahead and think for a minute . . . then I'd like to ask you why you chose them.

In his 1980 book *Loss*, drawing on work in cognitive science, Bowlby had highlighted the distinction between two forms of memory. 'Episodic' memories are those about specific events in the past. 'Semantic' memories are broad characterisations about how things tended to be. "When I was 7, there was this time I got lost in the park. I walked around calling out" likely draws on episodic memory because it is about a specific event. "They were always nice to me" likely draws on semantic memory because the account is a generalisation, not tied to a specific instance. Main and colleagues wanted to explore both episodic and semantic memories, so the protocol for the AAI included prompts both for general descriptions of relationships with caregivers and requests for specific memories that support the descriptions provided.

A first pattern observed by the researchers in the AAI transcripts was that some parents in the sample flatly described perfect childhoods. When asked to draw on semantic memory, participants characterised their attachment figures as good, caring, and loving. But when asked to supply episodic memories to support these descriptions, the participants said that they could not remember, or else produced contradictory memories. These participants were labelled 'dismissing' (Ds) since they appeared to be dismissing episodic information about their caregivers and attachment experiences, giving priority instead to overgeneralised and rather idealised accounts.

Particularly fascinating was that this dismissing pattern was especially common among parents from dyads who had been classified as avoidantly attached five years earlier in the Strange Situation.

A second pattern identified by the researchers was that some parents spoke about their attachment relationships with some attention to both positive and negative aspects, even if these relationships had been difficult. They were also able to support their general characterisations of their caregivers with memories of specific events, integrating semantic and episodic memory. These participants were labelled 'autonomous' (F), since they seemed free from "restrictions of varying types . . . placed on attention and the flow of information with respect to attachment."[2] These participants seemed able to recognise the importance of the relationships with their own caregivers. But they were also able to evaluate them. They offered well-balanced descriptions informed by awareness of the good and the bad in memories of specific events. The autonomous pattern was especially common among parents from dyads who had been classified as securely attached five years earlier in the Strange Situation.

A third pattern was that some parents in the AAI seemed focused on prosecuting a case against their caregivers. Generalised descriptions of their caregivers tended to be resoundingly negative or difficult to decipher. But when asked to supply episodic memories to support these descriptions, many of these participants entered into rambling narratives focused on specific grievances, losing track of the interviewer's question. Main and colleagues labelled these participants 'preoccupied' (E) since they appeared to be preoccupied with anger and frustration regarding episodes in their past and present relationships with attachment figures. Some parents with preoccupied speech had been part of dyads classified as resistant five years earlier in the Strange Situation, but there were rather few of these in the Berkeley sample.

The link between an infant's Strange Situation behaviour and his/her parent's autobiographical discourse is an intriguing finding. One interpretation of this link – a significant and quite widespread misunderstanding – has been that the Strange Situation is a measure of attachment, and the AAI is a measure of attachment, and so there is an association because the adult's 'attachment' gets passed on to the child. In fact, the AAI was definitely not intended as an assessment of attachment: it was given its name because it was an interview about attachment experiences.

Rather, Main and colleagues felt that the AAI measures individual differences in how individuals give attention to information about attachment-related experiences, expressed in their current 'states of mind' regarding attachment. In these terms, there seemed to Main and colleagues some profound similarities between how caregivers responded to the AAI and how their children responded to them in the Strange Situation. They proposed that "we may conceive of the AAI (like the Strange Situation) as creating conditions that arouse and direct attention toward attachment."[3]

In the Strange Situation reunion episodes, the infant in an avoidant attachment relationship directs attention rigidly towards the environment and away from the caregiver on reunion, to avoid showing distress and approaching the caregiver. Main and colleagues reflected that this seemed surprisingly similar to their parent in the AAI, keeping attention away from the actual events of their childhood and the feelings these memories would evoke. Autonomous speakers seemed to be able to attend to both semantic and episodic memories, and good and bad memories, in a free and flexible way, responsive to the questions being asked. This was like the infant from a secure dyad in the Strange Situation, who was free and flexible in turning attention to the toys or their caregiver, depending on what was going on. By contrast, preoccupied speech seemed to be analogous to the infant of a resistant dyad in the Strange Situation, who is "unable to direct attention to the environment, expresses strong and sometimes continual fear and distress, and seems constantly directed toward the parent".[4]

The AAI is, therefore, a peculiar assessment. The content of what speakers say or their actual history is not ultimately critical for their classification. What is important is whether there appears to be restrictions on information or incoherence in what the speaker says about their attachment relationships. AAI coders are required to make a judgement about whether the speaker's account of their upbringing seems internally consistent and well-supported by specific examples.

With some transcripts, it appears that negative episodic memories are being *dismissed or kept out of view* by idealisation of caregivers or difficulty with remembering or reporting on experiences. None of us recalls every event in our life. But if we have described our mother or father as a model for all parents, it would be surprising if we could not then offer some examples of what they had done well. In other transcripts, it appears that negative episodic memories have become a *preoccupying focus* of the speaker's attention. As a result, the speaker finds it difficult to attend to other questions asked by the interviewer. Sometimes interviewees go on about an event as if it is almost in the present for them, as if they are, even today, trying to work out what it means.

A contrast can be drawn between the AAI coding system and a different approach to analysing narratives, the 'attachment scripts' approach.[5] The attachment scripts coding system examines participants' assumptions about the availability of others when they need or have needed help or support. These expectations can be assessed in various ways. So, for instance, children may be presented with scenarios in which someone like them is confronted with an alarming situation, and they are asked what they would expect to happen then. Or AAI transcripts can be re-coded to focus on what the speaker's expectations appear to be about the availability of others when they need or have needed help or support. Some researchers have also examined the attachment scripts implicit in observed behaviour, for instance, in adult couples' communication with one another.[6]

EXTRACT FROM THE SCALES FOR SCORING SECURE BASE USE AND SUPPORT[7]

7. Very good secure base use

The individual has expressed his/her distress and need for help clearly initially and throughout the discussion. He/she appears fully confident (even when upset) that the partner should be responsive. By the end of the discussion the distressed individual appears more relaxed and satisfied.

3. Fair secure base use

a. The individual has not expressed his/her distress/need very well, and appears somewhat wary of making a full approach or seems concerned that the partner cannot really help him/her. He/she remains somewhat tense or distressed.

b. The subject has been fairly clear in expressing distress/need/concern, and for the most part he/she stays on topic throughout the session. The expectation that the partner can or should help is not clearly evident.

c. A verbally abusing careseeker should not get above a 3.

By contrast, the Main and colleagues coding system for the AAI was conceptualised as assessing individual differences in the direction of attention to attachment-relevant information. That said, few researchers have ever actually attempted to examine whether this is correct, so it remains somewhat unclear what exactly the AAI coding system actually measures, though clearly it is something to do with how individuals process information about attachment-related experiences.

One important reason that attachment researchers have been complacent about what the Adult Attachment Interview measures is that they have been fascinated by and focused on its empirical associations. One area of inquiry has been associations between the AAI and mental health difficulties. A meta-analysis by Madigan and colleagues found a considerable association between an insecure AAI classification and depression and anxiety ($r = 0.30$) and also an association with attention and conduct problems ($r = 0.22$).[8]

Another area of research that has especially fascinated attachment researchers has been associations between the AAI and the Strange Situation classifications assigned to the children of the interviewed parents. Studies have repeatedly supported this intriguing link. From a meta-analysis of 95 samples (4,819 caregiver-child dyads), Verhage and colleagues reported that autonomous (F) discourse and secure (B) infant attachment have an association of $r = .31$; dismissing (Ds) discourse and avoidant (A) infant attachment have an association of $r = .29$; and preoccupied (E) discourse and resistant (C) attachment have an association of $r = .22$.[9] In general, the association between the AAI and the Strange Situation was weaker for families facing specific risks and adversities ($r = .18$) and stronger for families recruited from the general population ($r = .38$).

These are quite substantial effect sizes for the social sciences, especially when we keep in mind that the AAI and Strange Situation are tremendously different kinds of assessment, applied to two different persons, and can be conducted many years apart. However, too often, people talk and write as if a match between AAI and Strange Situation classifications can more or less always be expected. That is not the case.

Regardless of an adult's AAI classification, the most likely classification for their child's attachment relationship is secure. For instance, among parents with dismissing (Ds) classifications, 40% of child-parent relationships were classified as secure (B), whereas 29% were classified as avoidant (A).[10] Child-parent relationships seem to have a tendency to *default to security*. This could be because conditional strategies are alterations of the basic functioning of the attachment

system. Or it could be that children are able to draw safe haven availability from their parent through their behaviour and, in doing so,
build expectations that their caregiver is available in times of need.

Another point to keep in mind is that, rather than simple lines
of correspondence between attachment patterns, dismissing and
preoccupied discourse is generally linked to insecure attachment
classifications of whatever kind. For instance, among parents with
preoccupied representations, 21% were part of dyads classified as
resistant in the Strange Situation, 22% disorganised, and 18% avoidant.[11] The relationship between the AAI classification and children's
expectations about safe haven availability appears to be more complex than one-to-one correspondence, as may inadvertently have
been suggested by the metaphor of attachment 'transmission' used by
researchers. It may also suggest, as Everett Waters has often argued,
that the important distinction to draw is between security and insecurity, with the distinction between avoidance and resistance somewhat less important.

Simplified stories also often assume that 'attachment' will be stable from infancy to adulthood and, on this basis, assume that there
is a strong correlation between the Strange Situation classification
and later AAI classification. In fact, a meta-analysis by Pinquart et al.
found no reliable associations between infant (including Strange Situation) and adult (including AAI) classifications.[12] However, they did
find evidence for moderate stability across shorter time spans (e.g.,
infancy to middle childhood; middle childhood to adulthood). They
also found evidence for stronger stability in samples recruited from the
general population than from samples recruited on the basis of specific
risks and adversities. Like Opie (Chapter 4), they confirmed stronger
continuity for secure than for insecure attachment classifications.

Attachment classifications are clearly somewhat stable over time.
And longitudinal research has documented that security in the Strange
Situation is robustly associated with positive adaptation and thriving
decades later ($r = .26$), even taking into account other features of participants' childhood experience.[13] However, these associations may
well not be based on the stability of a specific thing called 'attachment'

over time. More likely, early experiences of safe haven availability have a chain of positive consequences for an individual's well-being and flourishing, for instance, through supporting coherence of processing of attachment-relevant information or the availability of secure base scripts that help with trusting and relating to others.

LACK OF RESOLUTION

In addition to the three patterns of response in the Adult Attachment Interview described earlier, Main and colleagues also identified some interview transcripts where speech about a particular parent or other attachment figure was disrupted. They noted two associations. First, these disruptions particularly seemed to occur around experiences of bereavement. Though not all bereaved speakers showed such disruptions; it was only for some participants that thinking about the loss caused this disruption in their autobiographical accounts. Second, these speakers were frequently those who had been part of parent-child dyads in which the child was classified as showing disorganised attachment five years earlier.

Main and colleagues developed a coding system for these disruptions, which they termed 'lapses' in discourse. They distinguished two kinds, though these kinds may co-occur:

1. *Lapses in the monitoring of reasoning*: here the participant would speak about the lost attachment figure in ways that seemed physically or logically impossible. For instance, a speaker might imply that the dead person remains alive and involved in their life on a daily basis.

2. *Lapses in the monitoring of discourse*: here participants show interruptions in their capacity to respond in an appropriate way to the interviewer's questions, with the issue of death appearing where it had no obvious place, the speaker becoming absorbed in particular details surrounding the death unrelated to the question, or exceptionally long blank pauses that the speakers do not themselves seem to notice.

The Berkeley sample was selected to be low-risk, and the number of participants who had experienced significant trauma besides bereavement was relatively limited. However, as the AAI was used in additional samples, and particularly in cohorts drawn from clinical settings, Main and colleagues came to observe similar disruptions in the speech of some participants describing relationships with abusive caregivers. Again, not all speakers who had experienced abuse showed disruption in speech when talking about the abuse. Only some participants did. And again, these disruptions were associated with child disorganised attachment when the caregiver and child were observed in the Strange Situation.

Bowlby had characterised loss as potentially a kind of psychological trauma. Indeed, the first chapter of his book *Loss* is titled 'The trauma of loss'. This seemed to be supported by the fact that similar kinds of disruptions occurred in adult speech about both loss and abuse in the AAI. When coding an AAI, Main and colleagues therefore advised that the scoring of unresolved loss and unresolved abuse should be combined into one unresolved classification.

Using this combined classification for unresolved loss and abuse, researchers have found important associations with observations of caregiving behaviours. Schuengel and colleagues found that unresolved states of mind were associated with alarming caregiver behaviours, such as threatening the child or dissociative episodes.[14] These findings have been replicated by subsequent researchers, with a meta-analytic association of $r = .26$.[15]

Main wondered about the psychological process or processes underpinning lapses in reasoning and discourse in the AAI. She proposed that these lapses in adult speech about loss or trauma may not just be correlated with disorganised infant attachment in the Strange Situation but represent an equivalent psychological process of dissociation. That said, she has not tested this proposal. Nor have subsequent researchers, in part because Main and colleagues did not make especially specific claims about what disorganised/disoriented states of mind entail, which has made it harder to develop specific, testable hypotheses. One consequence has been that we still do not know much about how unresolved/disorganised states of mind relate to other standardised measures and conceptualisations of trauma and dissociation.[16]

An exception to this is replicated findings linking unresolved disorganised/disoriented states of mind to post-traumatic stress disorder and to higher scores on the Tellegen absorption scale, believed to capture milder forms of dissociation.[17] Another exception is that unresolved states have been empirically linked to outcomes such as addictive online gaming behaviour and mystical experiences, as mediated by facets of dissociation.[18] Thus, research does support Main and Hesse's hypothesis that trauma and dissociation/absorption are relevant, one way or the other, to understanding unresolved/disorganised/disoriented states.

Subsequent researchers have repeatedly supported the link between unresolved speech and disorganised infant attachment. However, the association has been less strong than Main and colleagues originally anticipated when they claimed that they were part of essentially the same process. Meta-analytic research with 95 samples (4,819 caregiver-child dyads) found an association of $r = .21$, which is still very notable, especially when considering that unresolved speech is usually identified only in a few speech passages or sentences across a 20–30-page transcript and disorganised attachment in a few seconds to minutes of behaviours in a 20-minute procedure. Nonetheless, this is the weakest of the associations between the AAI and the corresponding category in the Strange Situation.[19] Indeed, preoccupied speakers in the AAI are just as likely as unresolved speakers to be part of child-caregiver dyads in which the child's behaviour is classified as disorganised in the Strange Situation.[20]

ADOLESCENCE

Just as extending the Strange Situation to toddlerhood was an important step in building a toolkit for lifespan attachment research, the AAI has been adapted downward to adolescence to address this important developmental period. The situation of adolescents is, in many regards, not the same as for adults, and this has implications for their discussions of attachment-relevant memories. Though they may still live at home, adolescents' growing push for autonomy typically coincides with their increasing dependence on peers, typically romantic partners and friends. This means that peers can be sought as safe haven and used as a secure base under some circumstances, even while adolescents seek to establish some autonomy in relation to parents but also retain access to them in times of need.[21] Adolescence is sometimes a turbulent period in part because the individual may not always know where to find security and yet is confronted by new and larger developmental challenges than in childhood.

The Friends and Family Interview[22] is a version of the Adult Attachment Interview adapted to the specific life stage of adolescence. This includes the following:

- The kinds of challenges young participants may be facing, including potentially the need to manage the feelings or day-to-day coping of their own caregivers.
- Expectations about young people's capacities to recall and report on their experiences.
- The developmental challenges young people face in learning about the potential diversity of their feelings.
- Experiences with siblings and friends.

As well as looking for indications of dismissing, preoccupied, or unresolved states of mind, the Friends and Family Interview adds two further elements of analysis to the AAI. One is attention to the capacity of the young person to identify and reflect on their own thoughts and feelings about attachment relationships, and to identify and reflect on the experiences of others (see Chapter 7 on mentalising). Secondly, the Friends and Family Interview also has a scale for the extent to which the young person appears to perceive the availability of a safe haven and secure base in their relationships and, in this regard, also incorporates aspects of the 'attachment script' approach. Another adaptation of the AAI for a younger age group is the Child Attachment Interview.[23] However, data protection restrictions in the European Union have meant that the reliability materials can no longer be shared with trainees, and no trainings have run for several years.

Research by Decarli and colleagues offers an illustration of use of the Friends and Family Interview.[24] Using psychophysiological measures, they studied emotion-regulation among around 50 adolescents (11–17 years) during the Friends and Family Interview and in a parent-child conflict interaction task. Adolescents classified as unresolved/disorganised on the Friends and Family Interview had more difficulties down-regulating negative emotions, both during the interview itself and in the conflict interaction task. These findings are in line with the link between infant disorganised attachment and attentional and behavioural problems (Chapter 4).

NOTES

1 Waters, E., Vaughn, B.E., & Waters, H.S. (2021). *Measuring Attachment: Developmental Assessment Across the Lifespan*. New York: Guilford.

2 Main, M., Kaplan, N., & Cassidy, J. (1985). Security in infancy, childhood, and adulthood: A move to the level of representation. *Monographs of the Society for Research in Child Development*, 50, 66–104, p. 100.

3 Main, M. (1995). Recent studies in attachment: Overview, with selected implications for clinical work. In S. Goldberg, R. Muir, & J. Kerr (Eds.), *Attachment Theory: Social, Developmental and Clinical Perspectives* (pp. 407–470). Hillsdale, NJ: Analytic Press, p. 452.

4 Main, M., Kaplan, N., & Cassidy, J. (1985). Security in infancy, childhood, and adulthood: A move to the level of representation. *Monographs of the Society for Research in Child Development*, 50, 66–104, p. 74.

5 Waters, H., Waters, T., & Waters, E. (2020). From internal working models to script-like attachment representations. In R.A. Thompson, J.A. Simpson, & L. Berlin (Eds.), *Attachment: The Fundamental Questions* (pp. 111–119). New York: Guilford.

6 Crowell, J.A., Treboux, D., Gao, Y., Fyffe, C., Pan, H., & Waters, E. (2002). Assessing secure base behavior in adulthood: Development of a measure, links to adult attachment representations and relations to

couples' communication and reports of relationships. *Developmental Psychology*, 38(5), 679–693.

7 Crowell, J.A., Pan, H., Gao, Y., Treboux, D., & Waters, E. (1998). *Scales for Scoring Secure Base Use and Support from Couple Problem-Solving Interactions*. Unpublished Manuscript. Available at: https://psychology.psy.sunysb.edu/attachment/measures/content/SBSS_manual_v2_1998.pdf.

8 Madigan, S., Brumariu, L.E., Villani, V., Atkinson, L., & Lyons-Ruth, K. (2016). Representational and questionnaire measures of attachment: A meta-analysis of relations to child internalizing and externalizing problems. *Psychological Bulletin*, 142(4), 367–399.

9 Verhage, M.L., Schuengel, C., Madigan, S., Fearon, R.P., Oosterman, M., Cassibba, R., . . . van IJzendoorn, M.H. (2016). Narrowing the transmission gap: A synthesis of three decades of research on intergenerational transmission of attachment. *Psychological Bulletin*, 142(4), 337–366.

10 Madigan, S., Verhage, M.L., Schuengel, C., Fearon, P.R.M., Duschinsky, R., Roisman, G.I., . . . & The Collaboration on Attachment Transmission Synthesis. (in press). In search of patterns of cross-transmission from parental attachment representations to child attachment: An individual participant data meta-analysis. *Attachment & Human Development*.

11 Madigan, S., Verhage, M.L., Schuengel, C., Fearon, P.R.M., Duschinsky, R., Roisman, G.I., . . . & The Collaboration on Attachment Transmission Synthesis. (in press). In search of patterns of cross-transmission from parental attachment representations to child attachment: An individual participant data meta-analysis. *Attachment & Human Development*.

12 Pinquart, M., Feußner, C., & Ahnert, L. (2013). Meta-analytic evidence for stability in attachments from infancy to early adulthood. *Attachment & Human Development*, 15(2), 189–218.

13 Englund, M.M., Kuo, S.I.C., Puig, J., & Collins, W.A. (2011). Early roots of adult competence: The significance of close relationships from infancy to early adulthood. *International Journal of Behavioral Development*, 35(6), 490–496.

14 Schuengel, C., van IJzendoorn, M.H., Bakermans-Kranenburg, M.J., & Blom, M. (1998). Frightening maternal behavior, unresolved loss, and disorganized infant attachment: A pilot study. *Journal of Reproductive and Infant Psychology*, 16, 277–283.

15 Madigan, S., Bakermans-Kranenburg, M.J., Van IJzendoorn, M.H., Moran, G., Pederson, D.R., & Benoit, D. (2006). Unresolved states

of mind, anomalous parental behavior, and disorganized attachment: A review and meta-analysis of a transmission gap. *Attachment & Human Development*, 8(2), 89–111.

16 Bakkum, L., Oosterman, M., Verhage, M.L., Kunseler, F.C., Fearon, R.P., Schuengel, C., & Duschinsky, R. (2022). Psychophysiological responses underlying unresolved loss and trauma in the adult attachment interview. *Development and Psychopathology*, 34(1), 197–212; Bakkum, L., Schuengel, C., Foster, S.L., Fearon, R.P., & Duschinsky, R. (2022). Trauma and loss in the adult attachment interview: Situating the unresolved state of mind classification in disciplinary and social context. *History of the Human Sciences*, Advance online publication.

17 Stovall-McClough, K.C., & Cloitre, M. (2006). Unresolved attachment, PTSD, and dissociation in women with childhood abuse histories. *Journal of Consulting and Clinical Psychology*, 74(2), 219.

18 Schimmenti, A., Guglielmucci, F., Barbasio, C.P., & Granieri, A. (2012). Attachment disorganization and dissociation in virtual worlds: A study on problematic internet use among players of online role playing games. *Clinical Neuropsychiatry*, 9, 195–202. Granqvist, P., Hagekull, B., & Ivarsson, T. (2012). Disorganized attachment promotes mystical experiences via a propensity for alterations in consciousness (absorption). *The International Journal for the Psychology of Religion*, 22, 180–197.

19 Verhage, M.L., Schuengel, C., Madigan, S., Fearon, R.P., Oosterman, M., Cassibba, R., . . . van IJzendoorn, M.H. (2016). Narrowing the transmission gap: A synthesis of three decades of research on intergenerational transmission of attachment. *Psychological Bulletin*, 142(4), 337–366.

20 Madigan, S., Verhage, M.L., Schuengel, C., Fearon, P.R.M., Duschinsky, R., Roisman, G.I., . . . & The Collaboration on Attachment Transmission Synthesis. (in press). In search of patterns of cross-transmission from parental attachment representations to child attachment: An individual participant data meta-analysis. *Attachment & Human Development*.

21 Zeifman, D., & Hazan, C. (2016). Pair-bonds as attachments. Mounting evidence in support of Bowlby's hypothesis. In J. Cassidy & P. Shaver (Eds.), *Handbook of Attachment: Theory, Research, and Clinical Applications*, 3rd ed. (pp. 416–434). New York: Guilford.

22 Steele, H., & Steele, M. (2005). The construct of coherence as an indicator of attachment security in middle childhood: The friends and

family interview. In K.A. Kerns & R.A. Richardson (Eds.), *Attachment in Middle Childhood* (pp. 137–160). New York: Guilford.

23 Target, M., Fonagy, P., & Shmueli-Goetz, Y. (2003). Attachment representations in school-age children: The development of the Child Attachment Interview (CAI). *Journal of Child Psychotherapy*, 29(2), 171–186.

24 Decarli, A., Pierrehumbert, B., Schulz, A., Schaan, V.K., & Vögele, C. (2022). Disorganized attachment in adolescence: Emotional and physiological dysregulation during the friends and family interview and a conflict interaction. *Development & Psychopathology*, 34(1), 431–445.

FURTHER RECOMMENDED READING

Duschinsky, R. (2020). Mary Main, Erik Hesse and the Berkeley social development study. In *Cornerstones of Attachment Research*. Oxford: Oxford University Press.

Hesse, E. (2016). The adult attachment interview: Protocol, method of analysis, and empirical studies: 1985–2015. In J. Cassidy & P.R. Shaver (Eds.), *Handbook of Attachment: Theory, Research, and Clinical Applications*, 3rd ed. (pp. 553–597). New York: Guilford.

Verhage, M.L., Schuengel, C., Madigan, S., Fearon, R.P., Oosterman, M., Cassibba, R., . . . van IJzendoorn, M.H. (2016). Narrowing the transmission gap: A synthesis of three decades of research on intergenerational transmission of attachment. *Psychological Bulletin*, 142(4), 337–366.

6

EXPERIENCES IN CLOSE RELATIONSHIPS: ROMANTIC ATTACHMENT AND RELIGION

ROMANTIC ATTACHMENT

The attachment literature branches off in two distinct directions from adolescence onwards. As described in the previous chapter, one of these largely deals with adolescents' and adults' 'state of mind' regarding attachment-related experiences with childhood caregivers. This tradition originated in developmental and clinical psychology. Methodologically, research on attachment-related individual differences in this tradition largely clusters around the AAI and interviews inspired by the AAI, such as the Current Relationships Interview, which addresses individual differences in processing of attachment-relevant information about current romantic relationships.[1]

The second tradition originated in social and personality psychology, with a predominant focus on romantic relationships. Methodologically, pertinent research clusters around self-report questionnaires such as the Experiences in Close Relationships (ECR) scale. These two traditions of adult attachment theory and research largely developed side by side, in parallel, without much cross-referencing or mutual influence. In other words, there has been a major divide operating here, though this has been changing in recent years.

DOI: 10.4324/9781003020349-7

The tradition of attachment research in social and personality psychology began when Shaver, Bradshaw, and Hazan noted several striking resemblances between the child's attachment to caregivers and romantic partners' attachments to one another.[2] In both relationships, physical, non-verbal communication is key, for example, in prolonged eye contact, holding hands, caressing, and being caressed by the other. Involuntary or unexpected separations cause distress, and reunions following sustained separations are usually marked by joy. Loss of a parent or romantic partner through death is followed by intense mourning.

Like the child's relationships with caregivers, romantic relationships are also not attachments from day one but develop into attachments over time as a function of repeated interaction. Physical intimacy and sexuality appear to facilitate or speed up the formation of an attachment bond with romantic partners, via 'lust-and-trust' related neurohormones (e.g., vasopressin and oxytocin) released in the partner's presence.[3] Over time, the centrality of the sexual system for the relationship usually subsides, whereas the attachment and caregiving systems become more central. Gradually, the partner can ultimately take on the role of a safe haven to turn to in distress and a secure base from which to explore challenges in life. From a biological perspective, evolution may have co-opted the attachment system for functional use also in the context of adult pair-bonds.

Yet Shaver, Bradshaw, and Hazan were also mindful that romantic relationships cannot be understood on the basis of attachment theory alone. They serve multiple functions, including coordinating people's potential wishes for affection, reproduction, control, financial security, kinship traditions, etc. Human cultures display enormous variability in how spousal relationships are arranged, how fixed or fluid they are, how and whether gender roles are assigned, and how central or peripheral the provision of a secure base and safe haven – to partners, and to children – is within these relationships. In some cultures, for example, the Tswana of Botswana, biological fathers are providers, but they do not live with their wives or children, a situation quite unlike that of the more egalitarian Aka culture, in Central Africa, where fathers are quite close to their reproductive partners and provide plenty of care for their mutual offspring from infancy onwards.[4]

In making sense of the claims of Shaver and colleagues and later work in social and personality psychology, it is important to identify that though they use the same language drawn from Bowlby and Ainsworth, they give it a different meaning to researchers like Main in the developmental tradition. This split follows Bowlby's own ambiguity in his use of concepts (Chapter 1). The developmental tradition has tended to use concepts of 'attachment', 'security', 'safe haven', etc. to refer *narrowly* to a person's expectations about the physical and attentional availability of specific caregiver(s) in times of need. By contrast, the social and personality psychology tradition has tended to use the same words *broadly* to refer to an adult's ideas about the general availability of physical or symbolic comfort within close relationships.

To give an example: for developmental attachment researchers, insecure attachment means that a person does not trust that an attachment figure will be available in times of need unless they alter attention to attachment-relevant information, either through preoccupied focus or by minimising attention to sources of such information. For social and personality psychologists, insecure attachment means the general assumption that other people are not available for physical or symbolic comfort as needed. This assumption may, secondarily, result in changes to attention to information about the availability of others for comfort, but it is the belief or expectancy per se that is the central concern for social and personality psychologists.

Like Bowlby and Ainsworth, the two traditions have a common interest in how our assumptions about relationships shape our use of them as a safe haven and secure base, and how these assumptions can also influence other aspects of our lives. But it is easy to get tripped up by this common element and the fact that the two traditions use the same words. It would seem like they are talking about the same thing. In fact, they are not. Developmentalists more often focus on the form of attention to attachment-relevant experiences, whereas social and personality psychologists typically focus on the content of beliefs about attachment-relevant experiences.

The Strange Situation and the Adult Attachment Interview are believed to tap flexibility vs. inflexibility of attention with respect to information about the availability of specific loved ones in times of need. Measures from the social and personality psychology tradition ask individuals to report on behaviours, beliefs, and feelings that point to generalised schemas about how intimate relationships work. As might be expected, there is almost no correlation between these measures. In both cases, perceptions of the availability of a safe haven and secure base will shape emotion, thoughts, and behaviour. For instance, both predict adult behaviour when themes of tenderness, care, or concern are relevant. Such behaviour is shaped, likely in different ways, by the flexibility vs. inflexibility of attention to information about the availability of specific loved ones in times of need and by generalised schemas about close relationships.

ADULT ATTACHMENT STYLES

Today, the most widely used instrument by social and personality psychologists is the Experiences in Close Relationships, developed by Shaver and colleagues. This 36-item self-report questionnaire scale yields scores on two continuous insecurity dimensions, where security is represented by low scores on both dimensions.

The first factor is labelled Avoidance. It represents an assumption that attempts to achieve closeness with others will be counterproductive or get rebuffed. It is assessed through endorsement of items about behaviours, beliefs, and feelings suggesting either i) concern about closeness (e.g., "I get uncomfortable when someone wants to be very close to me") or ii) reluctance to depend on others or to disclose to them (e.g., "I find it difficult to allow myself to depend on romantic partners"). Avoidant assumptions about intimate relationships mean that the availability of others is sought less readily and less insistently, even in times of need.

The second factor is labelled Anxiety. It represents a lack of confidence in whether or not close others are available, entailing a need for vigilance. It is assessed through endorsement of items about behaviours, beliefs, and feelings suggesting either i) distress about the unavailability of the attachment figure ("I get frustrated when my partner is not around as much as I would like") or ii) worry about the strength and durability of the relationship (e.g., revised "I do not often worry about being abandoned"). Anxious assumptions about intimate relationships mean that the availability of others is monitored and sought more readily and insistently, and lowering the threshold for treating events as representing a time of need.

Research with the ECR has produced a large and theoretically coherent body of research – including many experimental studies using implicit and physiological measures and behavioural observations. Notable correlates of the two ECR scales include relationship satisfaction (i.e., insecurity is associated with lower satisfaction), partner matching (i.e., people who score high in insecurity match up with one another), and relationship longevity (i.e., couples in which one or both partners are insecure tend to last less long). Other correlates of avoidance and anxiety can be seen in emotion regulation (i.e., insecurity hinders flexible emotion regulation) and prosocial outcomes/altruism (i.e., insecurity is related to lower prosociality).

To give an example of a study using the ECR, Granqvist and colleagues recently found that individuals who scored low on anxiety and avoidance on the ECR displayed lower physiological stress responses (i.e., skin conductance) when smelling their partner's body odour (vs. other odours). In contrast, relatively insecure adults displayed higher physiological stress when smelling their partner's odour.[5]

To take another example: in a study by Mikulincer, Shaver, and colleagues, they asked participants to make a journal documenting their dreams each night and how challenging they had found the preceding day. Participants who scored high on Avoidance were more likely to report dreams in which there was no use of others as a safe haven or secure base. Participants who scored high on Anxiety were more likely to report dreams in which they wanted to be close to another person, especially following difficult days.[6]

In community samples, insecure attachment styles are associated with more mental health difficulties. Attachment anxiety is associated with concurrent report of depressive symptoms in community samples ($r = .39$), as to a lesser extent is avoidance ($r = .26$).[7] In clinical samples, researchers have found an association between insecure attachment styles and vulnerability to PTSD ($r = .17$).[8] However the nature of the association remains to be unpicked: the few available longitudinal studies suggest that PTSD contributes more to attachment style than attachment style does to vulnerability to PTSD.[9]

One of the important discoveries of the social and personality tradition of attachment research has been the effects of security priming: the activation of particular representations for participants using standardised stimuli. Part of the background to this area of inquiry is that across different relationships, we may operate with more or less insecure assumptions. Our attachment styles with our mother and father, for example, only have a modest association with our attachment style in our current romantic relationship ($r = .24$ and $r = .24$ for anxiety; $r = .17$ and $r = .12$ for avoidance).[10] Even if to some extent we have an overarching attachment style that proves our default, researchers have found that it is possible to bring out these non-dominant assumptions about relationships by using certain cues.

Presented with stimuli that make people think about togetherness, security, and love, participants may behave in a more secure way – both those who are secure and those who are insecure. For instance, a study by Mikulincer and Shaver found that both dispositional attachment style and the presence or absence of a security prime contributed to people's behaviour. Both contributed, in experimental studies, to altruism and tolerant behaviour towards out-groups.[11] Both were also found to contribute to more constructive responses to feeling hurt by a partner.[12]

In some other areas of social psychology, exciting research using primes has failed to replicate in later studies. This turns out not to be the case for security priming. In a meta-analysis of the first 120 attachment priming studies, effects have held up well across affective ($r = .30$), cognitive ($r = .22$) and behavioural outcomes ($r = .22$).[13] Effects were stronger when a security prime was used for participants with an insecure attachment style.

Research on security priming is a consequential development for the study of attachment. Developmental psychologists such as Bosmans and colleagues, inspired by this work, have also given increasing empirical attention to moment-to-moment responses to attachment-related stimuli, over and above more enduring attachment dispositions, leading to an exciting research agenda.[14]

In both social and developmental psychology, there has been growing acknowledgement that for too long, academic researchers have focused on studying individual differences among individuals with different attachment classifications, almost as if they had personality types. Research on priming highlights the importance of perceived safe haven and secure base availability within ordinary life, an issue that is part of the everyday experience of everyone. This was core to the theory developed by Bowlby and Ainsworth but only now is becoming reflected in methodology. For instance, the State Adult Attachment Measure has been developed by Gillath and colleagues, based on the Experience in Close Relationships Scale, to assess these more dynamic perceptions.[15] That said, an area that will need more research is whether changes as a result of repeated security priming have any longer-term implications. Initial results are interesting, though. For instance, Hudson and Fraley found that experience of a prime once a week for four months was associated with a reduction in attachment anxiety.[16]

In discussing the social and personality tradition of attachment research, we want to consider three claims about the measure that are repeated time and again but in fact need to be evaluated carefully. A first claim is that the Experiences in Close Relationships scale measures attachment security. As noted, security is inferred in the Experiences in Close Relationships measure when participants have a low score on both the avoidance and anxiety dimensions.

However, the scale does not have many items that effectively tap the low end of these dimensions. The authors of the measure themselves acknowledge that feeling understood, feeling validated, and feeling cared about are important aspects of security which the measure does not capture well.[17]

There has been growing recognition of this weakness to the ECR among social and personality psychologists, and some important attempts to adapt their work. For instance, the State Adult Attachment Measure assesses security, avoidance, and anxiety on independent scales. Empirical findings have accumulated that security predicts outcomes – for instance, a reduced likelihood of partner violence in a romantic relationship – over and above the absence of anxiety and avoidance.[18] Overall, the Experiences in Close Relationships scale can be regarded as relatively weak in its capacity to capture security, which will have hindered both research and theory for understanding the specific effects of assumptions about safe haven and secure base availability.

A second claim, often repeated, that in fact needs evaluation is that the avoidance dimension is characterised by a positive representation of the self and a negative representation of others, and the anxiety dimension is characterised by a negative representation of oneself and a positive representation of others. As with much of what is said about attachment, this is vaguely right and has a 'wrap-it-up-with-a-bow' feel to it. In fact, an avoidant attachment style is not actually associated with a genuinely positive model of the self but only with a desire to avoid acknowledging vulnerability. These are similar but not the same thing. An anxious attachment style is likewise not associated with a genuinely positive model of others but with representations of others as ultimately insensitive and inattentive to their needs.[19]

A third claim that needs to be evaluated is the idea that when individuals report both high avoidance and high anxiety, this can be considered 'fearful attachment', which is frequently described by social and personality psychologists as equivalent to disorganised attachment. What they have in common is the idea of psychological conflict between a desire for intimacy with an attachment figure and concern that bids for contact may be rebuffed. But there is no evidence of an empirical correlation between 'fearful attachment' and disorganised attachment.

Whilst the idea of 'fearful attachment' is officially on the books, it is in fact not a major part of the research programme. In general, social and personality psychologists have assumed, rightly or wrongly, that they just need to separately analyse the two dimensions and not test for any interaction between avoidance and anxiety. The lack of attention to fearful attachment perhaps lies in part in, and in turn has reinforced, a tendency among social and personality psychologists to study student and community samples for their research, rather than clinical populations or those facing adversities. Some social and personality psychologists have therefore looked for alternatives to the Experiences in Close Relationships measure when working with these populations. For example, Paetzold and colleagues have made a new self-report measure for assessing experiences of fear and conflict in attachment relationships.[20]

ATTACHMENT AND RELIGION/SPIRITUALITY

Attachment behaviours may be directed not just to an individual's regular, 'animate' attachment figures – most notably caregivers and, later in life, romantic partners and close friends – but also to a host of other surrogate relationship partners. Bowlby and Ainsworth briefly discussed the possibility that individuals who have been inadequately cared for, or whose regular attachment figures are currently unavailable for one reason or another, may select certain other persons or person-substitutes as surrogate targets for their attachment systems.

Bowlby wrote, on the use of attachment figures:

> Whenever the 'natural' object of attachment behaviour is unavailable, the behaviour can become directed towards some substitute object. Even though it is inanimate, such an object

frequently appears capable of filling the role of an important, though subsidiary, attachment 'figure'. Like the principal attachment figure, the inanimate substitute is sought especially when a child is tired, ill, or distressed.[21]

Bowlby exemplified such substitute objects with teddy bears, pacifiers, and comforting blankets.

The use of attachment surrogates by infants and toddlers is typically directed to concrete objects. However, from preschool age onwards, the cast of surrogate characters may come to include a whole new set of abstract, invisible, and non-corporeal (non-bodily) entities. Thus, as children experience themselves thinking and planning, and imagine the intentions of their social interaction partners, they may begin to apply these ideas to symbolic, human-like others. For example, the preschool child may start to elaborate and interact with imaginary companions. This imaginary capacity also means that the mind of the preschooler can be hyper-receptive to religious and spiritual ideas when they are presented by caregivers and other people in the child's immediate surroundings.[22]

Attachment theory and research were initially extrapolated to the psychology of religion by Lee Kirkpatrick.[23] A core assumption behind this application is that 'God' has evolved culturally and is used psychologically as a non-corporeal attachment figure by people. More specifically, Kirkpatrick anticipated that God may be used by the individual as an attachment-target to regulate states of insecurity and to achieve or maintain feelings of security – a kind of symbolic safe haven. Empirical research has generally supported this idea. Studies have found that religious believers engage in activities that support the feeling of being close to God, turn to God as a safe haven when distressed, and represent God as a secure base offering protection to their activities in the world.[24]

Research indicates that, from a developmental viewpoint, there are two general attachment-related pathways to religion/spirituality and to different modes of being religious/spiritual. First, via social (or cultural) learning, individuals who are secure with respect to attachment often come to adopt religious or non-religious standards that are similar to those held by their sensitive attachment figures in childhood. Supportive empirical evidence comes from studies showing heightened parent–offspring similarity in religiousness among study participants with memories of secure attachment histories with parents.[25] Also, presumably via generalising expectations from their attachment relationships, secure individuals often represent God as available in times of need. Researchers have found, for example, that for secure individuals, 'God' is more cognitively available as a safe haven following threat priming.[26]

Second, although the generalisation of working models complicates matters for individuals with an insecure attachment history, some insecure individuals may find in God a beneficial surrogate attachment figure, who may partially help them compensate for states of insecurity and other unsatisfactory attachments. In particular, insecure individuals may turn to God and religion when in turmoil severe enough to cause their conditional insecure strategies to break down. Evidence comes from research indicating that attachment insecurity is linked to sudden religious conversions occurring during life periods of emotional turmoil.[27] Additional evidence, regarding a link between unresolved/disorganised states and mystical experiences, was described in Chapter 5.

As a corollary of the attachment–religion connection, attachment theory may help us to understand why religion and mental health are connected. The overall connection between religion and mental health is usually positive, though modest, and occasionally negative. Contextual factors associated with heightened attachment activation (e.g., stress, low social welfare) typically increase the strength of the observed links between religion and mental health. Also, aspects of mental health (e.g., anxiety or freedom from worry) that are most notably affected by having a safe haven and secure base in one's life are particularly reliably linked to religion. Finally, the aspects of religion most consistently linked to mental health express attachment-components, including belief in a personal, benevolent God with whom the individual experiences a close and secure relationship.

NOTES

1   Crowell, J.A. (2021). Measuring the security of attachment in adults: Narrative assessments and self-report questionnaires. In R.A. Thompson, J.A. Simpson, & L.J. Berlin (Eds.), *Attachment: The Fundamental Questions* (pp. 86–93). New York: Guilford.

2   Shaver, P.R., Hazan, C., & Bradshaw, D. ([1988] 2021). The integration of three behavioral systems. In T. Forslund & R. Duschinsky (Eds.), *Attachment Theory and Research: A Reader* (pp. 74–90). New York: Springer.

3   Zeifman, D., & Hazan, C. (2016). Pair-bonds as attachments. Mounting evidence in support of Bowlby's hypothesis. In J. Cassidy & P. Shaver (Eds.), *Handbook of Attachment*, 3rd ed. (pp. 416–434). New York: Guilford.

4   Hewlett, B.S. (2000). Culture, history, and sex: Anthropological contributions to conceptualizing father involvement. *Marriage & Family Review*, 29(2–3), 59–73.

5   Granqvist, P., Vestbrant, K., Döllinger, L., Liuzza, M.T., Olsson, M.J., Blomkvist, A., & Lundström, J.N. (2019). The scent of security: Odor of romantic partner alters subjective discomfort and autonomic stress responses in an adult attachment-dependent manner. *Physiology & Behavior*, 198, 144–150.

6   Mikulincer, M., Shaver, P.R., Sapir-Lavid, Y., & Avihou-Kanza, N. (2009). What's inside the minds of securely and insecurely attached people? The secure-base script and its associations with attachment-style dimensions. *Journal of Personality and Social Psychology*, 97(4), 615–633.

7   Zheng, L., Luo, Y., & Chen, X. (2020). Different effects of attachment anxiety and attachment avoidance on depressive symptoms: A meta-analysis. *Journal of Social and Personal Relationships*, 37(12), 3028–3050.

8   Woodhouse, S., Ayers, S., & Field, A.P. (2015). The relationship between adult attachment style and post-traumatic stress symptoms: A meta-analysis. *Journal of Anxiety Disorders*, 35, 103–117.

9   E.g. Solomon, Z., Dekel, R., & Mikulincer, M. (2008). Complex trauma of war captivity: A prospective study of attachment and post-traumatic stress disorder. *Psychological Medicine*, 38(10), 1427–1434.

10 Fraley, R.C., Heffernan, M.E., Vicary, A.M., & Brumbaugh, C.C. (2011). The experiences in close relationships – relationship structures

questionnaire: A method for assessing attachment orientations across relationships. *Psychological Assessment, 23*(3), 615–625.

11 E.g. Mikulincer, M., Shaver, P.R., Gillath, O., & Nitzberg, R.A. (2005). Attachment, caregiving, and altruism: Boosting attachment security increases compassion and helping. *Journal of Personality and Social Psychology, 89*(5), 817–839.

12 Shaver, P.R., Mikulincer, M., Lavy, S., & Cassidy, J. (2009). Understanding and altering hurt feelings: An attachment-theoretical perspective on the generation and regulation of emotions. In A.L. Vangelisti (Ed.), *Feeling Hurt in Close Relationships* (pp. 92–119). Cambridge: Cambridge University Press.

13 Gillath, O., Karantzas, G.C., Romano, D., & Karantzas, K.M. (2022). Attachment security priming: A meta-analysis. *Personality and Social Psychology Review, 26*(3), 183–241.

14 Cuyvers, B., Verhees, M.W., van IJzendoorn, M.H., Bakermans-Kranenburg, M.J., Rowe, A.C., Ceulemans, E., & Bosmans, G. (2022). The effect of attachment priming on state attachment security in middle childhood. *The Journal of Early Adolescence, 43*(2), 164–193.

15 Gillath, O., Hart, J., Noftle, E.E., & Stockdale, G.D. (2009). Development and validation of a state adult attachment measure (SAAM). *Journal of Research in Personality, 43*(3), 362–373.

16 Hudson, N.W., & Fraley, R.C. (2018). Moving toward greater security: The effects of repeatedly priming attachment security and anxiety. *Journal of Research in Personality, 74*, 147–157.

17 Frias, M.T., Shaver, P.R., & Mikulincer, M. (2014). Measures of adult attachment and related constructs. In G.J. Boyle & D.H. Saklofske (Eds.), *Measures of Personality and Social Psychological Constructs* (pp. 417–447). Philadelphia, PA: Elsevier.

18 Spencer, C.M., Keilholtz, B.M., & Stith, S.M. (2021). The association between attachment styles and physical intimate partner violence perpetration and victimization: A meta-analysis. *Family Process, 60*(1), 270–284.

19 Simpson, J.A., Rholes, W.S., & Phillips, D. (1996). Conflict in close relationships: An attachment perspective. *Journal of Personality and Social Psychology, 71*(5), 899–914.

20 Paetzold, R.L., Rholes, W.S., & Kohn, J.L. (2015). Disorganized attachment in adulthood: Theory, measurement, and implications for romantic relationships. *Review of General Psychology, 19*(2), 146–156.

21 Bowlby, J. (1969/1982). *Attachment and Loss: Vol. 1. Attachment.* New York: Basic Books, p. 313.

22 Granqvist, P. (2020). *Attachment in Religion and Spirituality: A Wider View.* New York: Guilford.

23 Kirkpatrick, L.A., & Shaver, P.R. (1990). Attachment theory and religion: Childhood attachments, religious beliefs, and conversion. *Journal for the Scientific Study of Religion*, 29, 315–334.

24 Granqvist, P. (2020). *Attachment in Religion and Spirituality: A Wider View.* New York: Guilford.

25 Granqvist, P. (1998). Religiousness and perceived childhood attachment: On the question of compensation or correspondence. *Journal for the Scientific Study of Religion*, 37, 350–367.

26 Granqvist, P., Mikulincer, M., Gewirtz, V., & Shaver, P.R. (2012). Experimental findings on god as an attachment figure – normative processes and moderating effects of internal working models. *Journal of Personality and Social Psychology*, 103, 804–818.

27 Granqvist, P., & Kirkpatrick, L.A. (2004). Religious conversion and perceived childhood attachment: A meta-analysis. *International Journal for the Psychology of Religion*, 14, 223–250.

FURTHER RECOMMENDED READING

Granqvist, P. (2020). *Attachment in Religion and Spirituality: A Wider View.* New York: Guilford.

Mikulincer, M., & Shaver, P.R. (2016). *Attachment in Adulthood: Structure, Dynamics, and Change,* 2nd ed. New York: Guilford.

Zeifman, D., & Hazan, C. (2016). Pair-bonds as attachments. Mounting evidence in support of Bowlby's hypothesis. In *Handbook of Attachment: Theory, Research, and Clinical Applications,* 3rd ed. (pp. 416–434). New York: Guilford.

7

CURRENT CONCERNS IN ATTACHMENT RESEARCH

MENTALISATION AND PSYCHOTHERAPY

In Chapter 5 we described the creation of the Adult Attachment Interview by Main and colleagues. The first use of the AAI in England was by Miriam and Howard Steele, together with Peter Fonagy – three psychoanalytically trained clinicians. They initiated a longitudinal study, collecting AAIs with both parents before their child was born, then completing infant-mother Strange Situations when the children were 12 months old, and infant-father Strange Situations at 18 months. A remarkable finding was that an autonomous AAI classification, even conducted before a child was born, was effective in predicting child-parent attachment security ($r = .48$). By contrast, the Strange Situation was not predicted by either the parents' self-report regarding the quality of their marital relationship or by their respective conscious beliefs and attitudes towards parenting.[1]

Yet whilst coding the transcripts, Steele, Steele, and Fonagy were intrigued that parents seemed to differ in their capacity to consider the role of thoughts and feelings in their own intentions and behaviour and in the intentions and behaviour of attachment figures. Drawing from ideas from psychoanalytic theory about the importance of patient insight, they termed this capacity 'reflective

DOI: 10.4324/9781003020349-8

function'. They found that reflective function was more common among parents with an autonomous AAI classification, but there was considerable non-overlap. They also found that when reflective function was controlled for, the Main and colleagues AAI classifications were no longer significantly related to the Strange Situation classifications. From this finding they concluded that the AAI classifications predicted the Strange Situation essentially because of their association with reflective function.

As we saw in Chapter 3, Ainsworth had developed a concept of 'sensitivity', by which she meant the caregiver's capacity to perceive and to interpret accurately the signals and communications implicit in the infant's behaviour and, given this understanding, to respond to them appropriately and promptly. Ainsworth anticipated that sensitivity would be a fundamental predictor of child attachment security. Steele, Steele, and Fonagy perceived Ainsworth's concept of sensitivity as incredibly insightful. But they were also concerned by some key limitations to the concept, outlined in Chapter 3. In their view, sensitivity was associated with child attachment security because it was an indirect measure of the extent to which a parent was *attentive to the thoughts and feelings* of their child, could interpret these accurately, and could respond to them promptly and in an undistorted way.

A parent's capacity to consider the role of thoughts and feelings in their child's intentions and behaviour was not technically 'reflective function' since a parent does not primarily have an attachment to a young child: their role is to provide care to the child rather than to seek protection and comfort from the child, though of course sometimes this happens. As a result, Fonagy developed the more general term 'mentalising' to refer to the more general capacity of an individual to consider the role of thoughts and feelings in intentions and behaviour, including outside of attachment relationships.

The relationship between mentalising and attachment has been a current concern for researchers. Notably, Steele, Steele, and Fonagy argued that attachment security was also at best of secondary importance. True, the Strange Situation could predict aspects of later

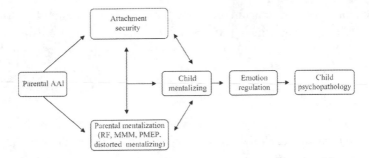

Figure 7.1 A model of factors hypothesised to relate to individual variations in parental mentalisation and suggested pathways for the development of psychopathology through mentalisation.

Source: Figure reprinted, with permission, from Sharp and Fonagy (2008)[2]

development, such as the development of aggressive behaviours or the quality of a child's relationships with peers. Yet, they argued that it was not expectations about attachment relationships that was driving these effects but rather the child's own developing capacity for mentalising, which would be facilitated by secure attachments.

Fonagy and collaborators have been outspoken in arguing that "the influence of attachment security on later development has nothing to do with representations of early relationships, and a futile search for this link has distracted attachment researchers."[3] Rather, he and his co-workers have advocated for the importance of a vicious cycle between problems in close relationships, difficulties with mentalising, and heightened negative emotions. This may or may not be true. We would flag, though, that in the two decades since making this proposal, there is yet to be evidence that when child mentalising is controlled for, there is no significant relationship between child attachment security and later outcomes.

A question that has, in fact, been examined is whether Steele, Steele, and Fonagy were right to suggest that it is reflective function, not sensitivity, that is fundamentally relevant for the development of attachment security. Zeegers and colleagues conducted a meta-analysis of the relative contributions of parental mentalising and sensitivity to child–caregiver attachment. They found that, even controlling for sensitivity, parental mentalising predicted child–caregiver attachment ($r = .24$). However they also found that, controlling for mentalising, sensitivity still predicted child–caregiver attachment ($r = .19$). These findings suggest that both processes are relevant, and neither is reducible to the other.[4]

Fonagy and collaborators have developed the idea of mentalising into an approach to psychotherapy, one that has become widely used. Versions of mentalisation-based therapy have been validated and delivered for patients with various mental health difficulties, for adults and for children, and as both individual and group therapy.[5] Particularly in the UK and Europe, mentalisation-based approaches have become embedded within national programmes. For instance, mentalisation-based therapy for antisocial personality disorder is delivered for patients identified with this condition across the Irish prison service.

The primary focus of mentalisation-based therapy is in supporting patients to be able to utilise the capacity to consider the role of thoughts and feelings in their own and others' intentions and behaviour. Fonagy and colleagues have proposed that a central obstacle to an individual's capacity to mentalise is activation of the attachment system by perceived threats, which make it difficult to pause to identify and reflect on thoughts and feelings. Patients in mentalisation-based therapy are taught about the conditional attachment strategies (Chapter 3) and encouraged to reflect on the ways in which their behaviour may at times resemble one of these patterns. The central therapeutic task is to help patients to retain their capacity to mentalise even in the stress and strain and urgency of attachment relationships and when conditional strategies are being elicited.[6]

As we saw in Chapter 2, Bowlby emphasised the role of the therapist as a secure base and safe haven for their client, permitting them to explore thoughts and feelings that would otherwise feel threatening. This has been an important idea for subsequent theory and research on attachment and psychotherapy. Researchers have found that improvements in attachment security during psychotherapy coincide with relief of symptoms ($r = 0.19$).[7]

Fonagy and colleagues claim, however, that this correlation does not imply that it was the improvements in attachment security that caused the relief of symptoms. Rather, they argue that the reduction in mental health difficulties is an effect of improvements in the capacity to consider the role of thoughts and feelings in intentions and behaviour, even in the highly activating context of attachment relationships. In their view, patients' security is only indirectly important, essentially a by-product of improved mentalising.

There have been several trials of mentalisation-based therapy. These have found that it has considerable effectiveness, competitive with other treatments for many conditions. For patients with complex personality disorders, mentalisation-based therapy appears from available evidence to be the most effective existing psychological treatment.[8] That said, no study to date has shown that it is improvements in mentalising, per se, that mediate the improvement in symptoms shown by patients who receive mentalisation-based therapy, as opposed, for instance, to the availability of the therapist as a secure base and safe haven. These questions of causality remain a current concern for researchers and have important implications for the priorities and approach of psychotherapeutic practice.

ATTACHMENT AND THE BRAIN

Claims about the impact of attachment on the developing brain have been common, especially in popular science books. In fact, the number of neuroscientific studies to have used validated measures of attachment or caregiving remains modest. Furthermore, studies have often been of populations, such as institutionalised children, who have had very different experiences to children brought up by families, even in maltreating homes.[9] There are as yet few well-replicated findings of the implications of attachment and caregiving for the brain in community samples.

One of the most rigorous and large-scale studies of attachment and the developing brain has been the Generation R study, in which 191 children were observed in free play with their parents at ages 1, 3, and 4. The sensitivity of both parents towards the child was coded by trained observers. At age 8, brain structure was assessed using magnetic resonance imaging (MRI). The results were striking. Controlling for the newborn's head size, higher levels of parental sensitivity in early childhood were associated with larger total brain volume (adjusted $b = 0.15$) and grey matter volume (adjusted $b = 0.16$) at age 8.[10] The researchers reported that there was no significant difference in predictive value between fathers' and mothers' observed sensitivity.

No significant associations were found between caregiver sensitivity and white matter, amygdala or hippocampal volumes. That is to say the researchers found no greater specific effect on some subcortical structures than others: the effect was general. This aligns with findings that have linked caregiver sensitivity to various aspects of development, including cognitive, behavioural, and social development. These findings are important in illustrating that it is not just constitutional factors, such as the child's genes, that underlie brain development. Environments, in this case the caregiver's sensitivity to the child, obviously also matter.

Whilst caregiver sensitivity was not associated with the structure or size of the amygdala, it did appear to alter the connection between the amygdala and the medial prefrontal cortex. The amygdala is understood to be involved in emotional states such as feeling alarmed or anxious; the medial prefrontal cortex plays a role in the use of cognition in regulating emotions. The researchers found that lower combined parental sensitivity and especially lower maternal sensitivity predicted accelerated connectivity between these two structures.[11]

The researchers proposed a possible explanation for these findings: children who experience insensitive care may need to develop a conditional strategy, which entails minimising (avoidance) or intensifying (resistance) attention to attachment-relevant information.

Accelerated connectivity between the amygdala and the medial pre-frontal cortex may be the architecture underpinning these strategies.

The Dutch team also looked at the associations of Strange Situation classifications to brain structure.[12] Here they had access to 551 participants. Children with avoidant or resistant attachment patterns did not differ from those who were securely attached in any brain outcome. This is an important finding in the context of over-strong claims that have circulated about the relevance of secure attachment for brain development, and also a sobering reminder that effects of parental sensitivity are by no means always mediated by child attachment security.

For children classified as showing disorganised attachment in infancy, by age 8, participants showed larger hippocampal volume, on both the left and right side. This finding remained robust when controlling for the child's IQ and emotional and behavioural problems. There were no other associations for disorganised attachment with specific or global brain measures.

One possibility is that hippocampal volume is the cause of disorganised attachment behaviour, for instance, in hindering a child's regulatory efforts.[13] However, it seems likely that the effects may also go the other way around, since other studies have shown that childhood trauma is associated with larger hippocampal volume.[14] The reasons why disorganised attachment and childhood trauma would be associated with a larger, rather than a smaller, hippocampus remain a current concern. One hypothesis has been that these experiences promote an accelerated development of the hippocampus, which would develop more gradually in typically developing children.

A curious finding comes from a study by van Hoof and colleagues of a mixed group of adolescents: a third with trauma experiences, a third with depression, and a third without clinical symptoms. This study found that unresolved attachment measured using the Adult Attachment Interview was associated with smaller left hippocampal volume. This finding remained even after controlling for the extent of mental health needs, puberty status, age, gender, and IQ.

At first sight, this seems to contradict the finding earlier from Generation R, which linked disorganised attachment to larger hippocampal volume. However, this assumes that disorganised attachment and unresolved status on the Adult Attachment Interview measure the same thing. Main has sometimes implied this. But caution is needed about the assumption, as we saw in Chapter 4. Vrtička and colleagues have been developing a theoretical framework for interpreting findings to date and developing a research agenda for future attachment research.[15] One intriguing aspect of this agenda is the prospect of understanding more about the aligned and non-aligned neurological correlates of disorganised attachment and unresolved states of mind.

To date, more studies have been conducted using social psychological measures of attachment (Chapter 6) than measures from the developmental tradition such as the Strange Situation or Adult Attachment Interview. A meta-analysis of the first twelve fMRI studies reported theoretically coherent associations with self-reported attachment styles. An avoidant attachment style was associated with reduced activation of the left inferior frontal gyrus when participants were presented with an emotional stimulus. This suggests some inhibition of processing of the emotional stimuli. By contrast, an anxious attachment style was associated with greater activation of the left side of the amygdala, which may suggest greater concern with the emotional stimuli. These findings align with the wider literature using social psychological measures and an assessment of neurological activity, which offers a convergent picture: anxious attachment is associated with neurological activation around vigilance and threat, whereas avoidant attachment is associated with suppression of distress and of social reactivity.[16]

ATTACHMENT-BASED INTERVENTIONS

Finally, a third current concern in attachment research is the development and evaluation of caregiving interventions to support families. There are many forms of family intervention inspired by attachment research, and we cannot summarise them all. The interested reader is referred to the *Handbook of Attachment-Based Interventions*.[17] However, we highlight a few aspects of this work here.

Parenting is an extremely multifaceted process. And when things are not going well, there tend to be vicious cycles. The premise of attachment-based interventions is that, despite this complexity, it is possible to support change in parenting behaviours relevant to the child's expectations of the availability of the caregiver as a safe haven in times of need. But what aspect of family life should be the priority for intervention to achieve this?

In the 1990s, Bakermans-Kranenburg and colleagues conducted an important meta-analysis of existing interventions to lay the groundwork for a refined answer to this question.[18] One argument that had been put forward was that there should not be any focus to the intervention: if families are complex, interventions should address family life as a whole in order to impact a child's experience of the caregiver's availability. However, Bakermans-Kranenburg and colleagues found the opposite: all interventions that attempted to make a comprehensive and holistic intervention in the lives of families either had no effect on patterns of attachment or, actually, increased insecurity. By contrast, interventions with a more specific focus had a greater positive effect.

Another argument had been that in the context of economic adversity, interventions with a specific focus would be less effective given the other demands on caregivers' coping. In fact, Bakermans-Kranenburg found that parenting interventions in the context of economic adversity were no less effective, and subsequent work by Facompré has shown that, in fact, they are more effective at reducing disorganised attachment in a context of economic adversity.[19]

One potential point of departure for a specific intervention, discussed in Chapter 3, stems from the idea that sensitive caregiver behaviour contributes to secure attachment. When a caregiver's behaviour shows awareness and responsiveness to their child's concerns, this can be anticipated to contribute to the child's expectation that the caregiver is available as a safe haven. It can also be anticipated to help give the child confidence to use the caregiver as a secure base from which to explore, since they know their signals will be heard and addressed if they need help.

This point of departure for intervention has been the particular focus of an intervention called Video-feedback Intervention to promote Positive Parenting and Sensitive Discipline (VIPP-SD), developed by Bakermans-Kranenburg, Juffer, and van IJzendoorn. VIPP-SD entails 6–8 1½ hour sessions of video-feedback with parents at home. The caregiver and child are filmed during ordinary interaction. These recordings are screened for suitable moments to highlight strengths shown by the caregiver in demonstrating sensitive care, as well as opportunities for further development of this skill. The intervention builds precisely on the caregiver's *own* expertise, with the caregiver serving as a reinforcing role model for themselves.

As well as supporting sensitive care, a target for the intervention is to support sensitive discipline of the child when needed. This focuses on helping the caregiver avoid the need to be coercive, provide positive reinforcement, deescalate when the child is becoming frustrated, and achieve empathy for the child and consistent limit-setting. A meta-analysis of the first 25 randomised controlled trials of VIPP-SD found an effect size of $r = .18$ for changes in parenting behaviour and $r = .23$ for changes in attachment security. Researchers have found no indication of a decrease in effect size stemming from length of follow-up, suggesting that effects of the intervention remain stable over time.[20] Change over time in caregiver sensitivity was very strongly associated with change in child attachment security ($r = .50$), affirming the importance of sensitivity as the mechanism targeted by VIPP-SD.

Curiously, trials of VIPP-SD have found that it also reduces the likelihood of disorganised infant-caregiver attachment. This is a puzzle, since VIPP-SD focuses on improving caregiver sensitivity, but caregiver insensitivity is only weakly associated with disorganised attachment. This is a topic of active discussion among attachment researchers.

VIPP-SD has been widely used as a tool for supporting families facing difficulties. A recent further application of VIPP-SD has been as a tool for assessment. In social welfare contexts, professionals are interested in parents' capacity to change their behaviour. However, the measures developed by attachment researchers, such as the Ainsworth Strange Situation and sensitivity scale, have been validated only for understanding group-level processes. They inform us in important ways about what tends to happen prior to or following experiences of care, and so may be relevant in informing supportive work with families.[21] However, we do not yet know much about whether they can assess individuals with sufficient precision and better than whatever assessment-as-usual would otherwise be.

As mentioned in Chapter 4, Madigan and colleagues are in the process of assessing whether the AMBIANCE can be used effectively by practitioners in their assessments. Another approach has been to examine caregivers' response to the VIPP-SD, which may be able to offer insight into a caregiver's capacity to improve their parenting. For instance, Cyr and colleagues conducted a study with families known to child protection services for substantiated history of child maltreatment. A parenting capacity assessment was undertaken to examine whether the children needed to be removed. In half the cases, this assessment also included delivery of VIPP-SD; in the other half, the assessment included a general supportive and educational intervention.

Though there was most improvement for the group who received VIPP-SD, in both cases, the intervention contributed to improved scores on the parenting capacity assessment and also to the court's placement decision. However, only in the case of the assessment that included response to VIPP-SD was the evaluation predictive of re-reports of child maltreatment after a year. These findings suggest that assessment of response to VIPP-SD is valuable in giving information about a family's potential capacity to safely look after their child. The researchers suggest that VIPP-SD may achieve this by improving professionals' awareness of insensitive and alarming caregiving behaviour, improving family openness, and/or by helping professionals assess caregiver mentalising.[22] The use of attachment-based parenting interventions for dynamic assessment is an important development for attachment research, though more studies will be needed to adequately scope its validity and feasibility for applied work with families.

Whereas VIPP-SD focuses on caregiver sensitivity, a slightly different target for intervention has been adopted by the Attachment & Biobehavioural Catchup (ABC) intervention, developed by Dozier and colleagues. Here, coaches use video-feedback and in-the-moment feedback as the parent and child play. The feedback does not seek to enhance sensitivity in general but focuses on two particular aspects: helping the caregiver be nurturing when their child is distressed, and following the child's lead rather than dictating activities to them. Dozier regards these as the key lessons of Bowlby and Ainsworth, respectively. Additionally, ABC seeks to help caregivers avoid harsh or alarming behaviours. They regard this as a key lesson from Main and colleagues. Like VIPP-SD, ABC has also been demonstrated to contribute to increased caregiver sensitivity, greater infant–caregiver attachment security and less disorganised attachment, and fewer child behavioural problems.[23]

Dozier and colleagues regard ABC as a targeted intervention for parenting, which should be delivered alongside targeted interventions for other difficulties families are facing, for instance, parental substance use or insecure housing. However, it is currently unknown which such contextual factors impact the likelihood of success for the intervention. Furthermore, interventions to improve children's expectations of a safe haven will likely have knock-ons, whether positive or negative, elsewhere in the family system, for instance, in the relationship between caregivers. This remains a current key interest for research on attachment-based interventions.

NOTES

1 Fonagy, P., Steele, M., Moran, G.S., Steele, H., & Higgitt, A.C. (1991). Measuring the ghost in the nursery: A summary of the main findings of the Anna Freud Centre/University College London parent-child study. *Bulletin of the Anna Freud Centre*, 14, 115–131.

2 Sharp, C., & Fonagy, P. (2008). The parent's capacity to treat the child as a psychological agent: Constructs, measures and implications for developmental psychopathology. *Social Development*, 17(3), 737–754.

3 Fonagy, P., & Target, M. (2002). Early intervention and the development of self-regulation. *Psychoanalytic Inquiry*, 22(3), 307–335, p. 328.

4 Zeegers, M.A., Colonnesi, C., Stams, G.J.J., & Meins, E. (2017). Mind matters: A meta-analysis on parental mentalization and sensitivity as predictors of infant – parent attachment. *Psychological Bulletin*, 143(12), 1245–1272.

5 Bateman, A., & Fonagy, P. (2019). *Handbook of Mentalising in Mental Health Practice*, 2nd ed. Washington, DC: American Psychiatric Association.

6 Fonagy, P., & Adshead, G. (2012). How mentalisation changes the mind. *Advances in Psychiatric Treatment*, 18(5), 353–362.

7 Levy, K.N., Kivity, Y., Johnson, B.N., & Gooch, C.V. (2018). Adult attachment as a predictor and moderator of psychotherapy outcome: A meta-analysis. *Journal of Clinical Psychology*, 74(11), 1996–2013.

8 Kvarstein, E.H., Pedersen, G., Folmo, E., Urnes, Ø., Johansen, M.S., Hummelen, B., . . . Karterud, S. (2019). Mentalization-based treatment or psychodynamic treatment programmes for patients with borderline personality disorder – the impact of clinical severity. *Psychology and Psychotherapy: Theory, Research and Practice*, 92(1), 91–111.

9 Sheridan, M.A., Fox, N.A., Zeanah, C.H., McLaughlin, K.A., & Nelson, C.A. (2012). Variation in neural development as a result of exposure to institutionalization early in childhood. *Proceedings of the National Academy of Sciences*, 109(32), 12927–12932.

10 Kok, R., Thijssen, S., Bakermans-Kranenburg, M.J., Jaddoe, V.W., Verhulst, F.C., White, T., . . . Tiemeier, H. (2015). Normal variation in early parental sensitivity predicts child structural brain development. *Journal of the American Academy of Child & Adolescent Psychiatry*, 54(10), 824–831.

11 Thijssen, S., Muetzel, R.L., Bakermans-Kranenburg, M.J., Jaddoe, V.W., Tiemeier, H., Verhulst, F.C., . . . Van IJzendoorn, M.H. (2017).

Insensitive parenting may accelerate the development of the amygdala – medial prefrontal cortex circuit. *Development & Psychopathology*, 29(2), 505–518.

12 Hidalgo, A.P.C., Muetzel, R., Luijk, M.P., Bakermans-Kranenburg, M.J., El Marroun, H., Vernooij, M.W., . . . Tiemeier, H. (2019). Observed infant-parent attachment and brain morphology in middle childhood – A population-based study. *Developmental Cognitive Neuroscience*, 40, 100724.

13 Nolvi, S., Rasmussen, J.M., Graham, A.M., Gilmore, J.H., Styner, M., Fair, D.A., . . . Buss, C. (2020). Neonatal brain volume as a marker of differential susceptibility to parenting quality and its association with neurodevelopment across early childhood. *Developmental Cognitive Neuroscience*, 45, 100826.

14 Tupler, L.A., & De Bellis, M.D. (2006). Segmented hippocampal volume in children and adolescents with posttraumatic stress disorder. *Biological Psychiatry*, 59(6), 523–529.

15 White, L.O., Schulz, C.C., Schött, M., Kungl, M.T., Keil, J., Borelli, J.L., & Vrtička, P. (2020). A social neuroscience approach to interpersonal interaction in the context of disruption and disorganization of attachment. *Frontiers in Psychiatry*, 11, 1437.

16 Long, M., Verbeke, W., Ein-Dor, T., & Vrtička, P. (2020). A functional neuro-anatomical model of human attachment (NAMA): Insights from first-and second-person social neuroscience. *Cortex*, 126, 281–321.

17 Steele, H., & Steele, M. (Eds.). (2017). *Handbook of Attachment-Based Interventions*. New York: Guilford.

18 Bakermans-Kranenburg, M.J., Van IJzendoorn, M.H., & Juffer, F. (2003). Less is more: Meta-analyses of sensitivity and attachment interventions in early childhood. *Psychological Bulletin*, 129(2), 195–215.

19 Facompré, C.R., Bernard, K., & Waters, T.E. (2018). Effectiveness of interventions in preventing disorganized attachment: A meta-analysis. *Development & Psychopathology*, 30(1), 1–11.

20 Van IJzendoorn, M.H., Schuengel, C., Wang, Q., & Bakermans-Kranenburg, M.J. (2022). Improving parenting, child attachment, and externalizing behaviors: Meta-analysis of the first 25 randomized controlled trials on the effects of video-feedback intervention to promote positive parenting and sensitive discipline. *Development & Psychopathology*, 35(1), 241–256.

21 Steele, H., & Steele, M. (Eds.). (2008). *Clinical Applications of the Adult Attachment Interview*. New York: Guilford; Forslund, T., Granqvist, P., van IJzendoorn, M.H., Sagi-Schwartz, A., Glaser, D., Steele, M., . . . Duschinsky, R. (2022). Attachment goes to court: Child protection and custody issues. *Attachment & Human Development*, 24(1), 1–52.

22 Cyr, C., Dubois-Comtois, K., Paquette, D., Lopez, L., & Bigras, M. (2022). An attachment-based parental capacity assessment to orient decision-making in child protection cases: A randomized control trial. *Child Maltreatment*, 27(1), 66–77.

23 Dozier, M., & Bernard, K. (2019). *Coaching Parents of Vulnerable Infants: The Attachment and Biobehavioral Catch-Up Approach*, New York: Guilford.

FURTHER RECOMMENDED READING

Duschinsky, R., & Foster, S. (2021). *Mentalizing and Epistemic Trust*. Oxford: Oxford University Press.

Long, M., Verbeke, W., Ein-Dor, T., & Vrtička, P. (2020). A functional neuro-anatomical model of human attachment (NAMA): Insights from first-and second-person social neuroscience. *Cortex*, 126, 281–321.

Steele, H., & Steele, M. (Eds.). (2017). *Handbook of Attachment-Based Interventions*. New York: Guilford.

8

CONCLUSION

In this conclusion we survey some of the misconceptions about attachment discussed over the preceding chapters. We discuss some factors we suspect may be involved in producing these misconceptions. The chapter closes by identifying what we perceive as some critical questions for the future of the field.

A BALANCED PERSPECTIVE

Attachment theory and research have potential relevance across a wide variety of domains. Yet the theory as well as its surrounding research and applications are also controversial. Uncritical advocates for attachment theory have claimed that attachment relationships have overriding importance for a child's development and their behaviour into adulthood. Unqualified critics have argued that attachment theory is overblown, and that attachment has relatively little importance for child development and later behaviour. Both sides can cite empirical studies in support of their positions.

In attempting to introduce the current state of knowledge from attachment research in this book, we have given particular priority to meta-analytic research where available. Meta-analysis draws together the results of different studies and offers a more encompassing picture, and often a less extremely positive or negative one.

DOI: 10.4324/9781003020349-9

Findings from meta-analytic research qualify over-strong claims for the causal importance of attachment relationships and show how factors like family adversity may impact main effects. However, findings from meta-analytic research also qualify over-strong claims about the irrelevance of attachment relationships, documenting important associations between a child's development and their access to a caregiver experienced as a safe haven in times of need.

In departing from the overall sway of evidence, and cherry-picking the studies they cite, extreme positions discussing attachment theory and research often present partial or inaccurate accounts. This is facilitated by the confusions about attachment that we have attempted to address in this book. For instance, we highlighted that Bowlby used the term 'attachment' in a narrow sense to mean seeking a safe haven with a caregiver, and in a broad sense to mean the child's general relationship with their caregiver (Chapter 1). Claims about the importance or irrelevance of attachment can use the same term 'attachment', cite Bowlby, and cite empirical evidence — but be talking about two profoundly different things. It is quite a muddle.

Popular advocates and critics of attachment also frequently seem to be operating with an outdated image. They appear unaware of the emphasis given by contemporary attachment research to the idea of the 'attachment network' (Chapter 2), or to the predictive significance of caregiver sensitivity compared to child attachment (Chapter 3). Where they do identify the importance of sensitivity, they often fail to recognise that the term was given a technical meaning by Ainsworth, not aligned with the ordinary connotations of the term (Chapter 3). Nor is it widely known that contemporary attachment researchers have refined the sensitivity construct, to focus on the caregiver's response to their child's distress, which is especially important for experiences of a safe haven in times of need (Chapter 3). Or that many contemporary attachment researchers have emphasised other factors besides sensitivity, including alarming caregiver behaviour (Chapter 4) and caregivers' attention to children's intentions, thoughts, and feelings (Chapter 7).

Among advocates and critics, and among many researchers too, there are multiple, widespread misunderstandings of the concept of disorganised attachment (Chapter 4). These include what the concept means, how exactly disorganised attachment is assessed in infants, toddlers, and older children, what association it has with the care a child has received, what prediction it offers for a child's later outcomes, and the role of factors like socioeconomic circumstances in altering this prediction. In particular, advocates have overstated the value of the disorganised attachment classification as an index of child maltreatment. Critics have assumed that the four-category system is arbitrary, failing to perceive the logic of the theory of attention to attachment-relevant information that underpins all of Main's work.

Advocates frequently make extreme claims about 'transmission' of 'attachment' from one generation to another, based on initial studies using the Adult Attachment Interview. In fact, the Adult Attachment Interview was not intended by Main as a measure of attachment: it is a system for coding adults' 'states of mind' regarding attachment in interviews about attachment experiences (Chapter 5). This coding system assesses the flexibility vs. rigidity of attention to attachment-relevant information. Associations between the Adult Attachment Interview and children's expectations of safe haven availability as measured by the Strange Situation are remarkable and highlight the significance of these attentional processes for caregiving. But the associations are also moderate in size and not necessarily straightforward. Regardless of an adult's Adult Attachment Interview classification, the most likely classification for their child's attachment relationship is secure. And rather than simple lines of correspondence between attachment patterns, dismissing and preoccupied discourse is generally associated with insecure attachment classifications of whatever kind.

A further source of confusion between researchers and in the reception of research about attachment has been the division between traditions of inquiry from developmental psychology and from social and personality psychology (Chapter 6). Advocates have described measures such as the Experiences in Close Relationships scale as measuring 'adult attachment'. Again, this is misleading. In fact, it is an assessment that asks participants to report on behaviours, beliefs, and feelings that point to generalised schemas about how intimate relationships work and what this means for the individual. However, it relates to attachment theory because a crucial part of such schemas is assumptions about one's safe haven and secure base availability.

Both popular advocates and critics have overemphasised how important the stability of classifications over time is for attachment theory. Advocates have often made claims about how attachment relationships rewire the brain. Certainly, sensitivity and attachment do seem to have notable associations with neurological observations – but the evidence base remains limited and is far from straightforward. Furthermore, it is important to recognise that attachment classifications are only moderately stable over time. However, such change is explicable in terms of theory. Caregiving predictably becomes less sensitive and attachment less secure in environments of adversity. Interventions that reduce insensitive and alarming caregiver behaviours can help support positive caregiving behaviour and child attachment (Chapter 7).

THREE PRINCIPLES

We have written this book inspired by a strong sense of the value of attachment theory and research. We have tried to convey the rigour and quality of the best work in this area, the ingenuity of developments in attachment theory and research which have evolved the field over time, and the dependability of key findings from convergent results studied in meta-analytic research.

We have aimed to offer a balanced perspective. Within the space available, we have tried to introduce attachment research as a rich, three-dimensional area of inquiry, with both strengths and weaknesses. In contrast to the idealised accounts of uncritical advocates, and the denigrating accounts of unqualified critics, it has been our hope that this book has offered a brief account of attachment theory and research, mindful of limitations in both current evidence and theory but also marking their genuine capacity for insight.

The chapters of this book have addressed what we perceive to be some of these central insights. Attachment theory and research has highlighted how important it is for us to feel we have access to a safe haven and secure base, and that we get greater benefit when we have more than one such relationship. It has identified individual differences in attachment, documenting how even young children may use intensification or minimisation of displays of distress to manage their relationship with caregivers.

Attachment research has documented the importance of sensitive care for supporting children's perception of the availability of a safe haven and secure base, and for their later development. Yet other factors have also been identified as important, including the caregiver's capacity to consider their child's perspective. It has also documented the significance of alarming caregiving behaviour for hindering children's perceptions that caregivers can be turned to in times of need. Children's perceptions of caregiver availability are associated with later outcomes across various domains including mental health, social relationships, neurological, and linguistic and cognitive outcomes. However, researchers have documented that perceptions about caregiver availability can change over time, especially when there are changes in caregivers' behaviour or the family situation. This point has been reinforced by studies of interventions to support parents which have been based on ideas from attachment theory.

Looking beyond childhood, researchers in developmental psychology have documented how adults may experience distortions in processing of attachment-relevant information, and important associations between these distortions and adults' mental health and parenting behaviour. Researchers in social psychology have also documented how adults' perceptions of how intimate relationship work can impact varied aspects of their lives, from love-relationships to religious practices.

In closing, we highlight a fundamental idea stemming from attachment theory and research. Appeal to attachment is often used to argue for the general value of supportive relationships for children, drawing on Bowlby's broader use of the term (Chapter 1).

Yet beyond this general claim, empirical research has documented the specific value of attachment in the narrow sense of the term: *the importance of relationships with familiar figures that provide expectations of safe haven availability.* In a recent international consensus statement, this fundamental idea has been set out as three principles:[1]

- The development of attachment relationships, and the benefits for psychosocial development that may stem from these relationships, depend on experiences of safe haven provision by particular, familiar, and non-abusive caregivers.
- Expectations about safe haven availability stem from particular relationships and are not simply transferrable. Extreme caution should therefore be exercised in disrupting children's attachment relationships.
- Additional attachment relationships can be an asset for children. They do not typically disturb existing attachments unless they represent a source of threat or block access to existing relationships.

We regard this fundamental idea – the importance of relationships with familiar figures that provide expectations of safe haven availability – as a profound contribution, with great relevance across many areas of human life. It has a great deal further left to teach us – and with exciting questions still to be investigated.

NOTES

1 Forslund, T., Granqvist, P., van IJzendoorn, M.H., Sagi-Schwartz, A., Glaser, D., Steele, M., . . . Duschinsky, R. (2022). Attachment goes to court: Child protection and custody issues. *Attachment & Human Development*, 24(1), 1–52.

FURTHER RECOMMENDED READING

Forslund, T., Granqvist, P., van IJzendoorn, M.H., Sagi-Schwartz, A., Glaser, D., Steele, M., . . . Duschinsky, R. (2022). Attachment goes to court: Child protection and custody issues. *Attachment & Human Development*, 24(1), 1–52.

Thompson, R.A., Simpson, J.A., & Berlin, L.J. (Eds.). (2021). *Attachment: The Fundamental Questions*. New York: Guilford.

Waters, E., Vaughn, B.E., & Waters, H.S. (2021). *Measuring Attachment: Developmental Assessment Across the Lifespan*. New York: Guilford.

APPENDIX: KEY CONCEPTS

From: Society for Emotion and Attachment Studies (2021) Explanations of attachment theoretical concepts. Version April 2021. https://seasinternational.org/explanations-of-attachment-theoretical-concepts/

Attachment anxiety (Chapter 6): A set of schemas about close relationships entailing concern about abandonment, intense desire for reassurance from others, and distress and frustration about the perceived unavailability of others.

Attachment avoidance (Chapter 6): A set of schemas about close relationships entailing discomfort with closeness or reliance on others.

Attachment behaviour (Chapter 1): Any behaviour can be an attachment behaviour when it is directed towards gaining and maintaining the availability of an attachment figure when the attachment system is active. It is not an 'instinctual' preset pattern of behaviour. The expression of attachment behaviour can vary between situations and developmental stages. In infancy, common attachment behaviours include smiling, crawling towards the caregiver, reaching and clinging, and directed cries to attract the caregiver's attention.

Attachment figure (Chapter 1): An attachment figure is a familiar person who an individual wishes to use as a safe haven when the attachment system is activated and as a secure base for exploration when the attachment system is less activated. However, these response may be obstructed, for instance, in insecure (avoidant and resistant) attachment relationships (Chapter 3).

Attachment relationship (Chapter 1): A relationship between an individual and another person who functions as an attachment figure for the individual. As long as a caregiver is sufficiently familiar and the relationship sufficiently stable over time, children will develop an attachment relationship with this caregiver. An attachment relationship may exist even if the attachment figure is rejecting or abusive. The quality of the care provided does not determine whether or not an attachment relationship develops, but rather shapes whether the attachment relationship is secure or insecure. This also means that a child can form multiple attachment relationships with different attachment figures.

Attachment system (Chapter 1): The 'attachment system' describes the motivation to seek the availability of attachment figures. The attachment system is thought to be 'activated' when an individual is distressed, frightened, tired, or ill, which may not always be visible in the individual's behaviour (see avoidant attachment). This motivation has a basis in evolution and, on this basis, is especially easy for humans to develop. However, it is misleading to think of attachment as an 'instinct', because experiences with the attachment figure shape whether, when, and how the system becomes activated and effectively deactivated by seeking contact with the attachment figure. The goal of the attachment system is to achieve and maintain the availability of the attachment figure as a safe haven and secure base. In infancy, this goal may be set as achievement of both attentional availability and responsiveness of the caregiver; the degree of availability sought will depend on the extent of the activation of the system. In adulthood, the goal of the attachment system may be set in ways that make use of capacities for communication and cognitive abstraction, for instance, thinking about a loved one or symbolic entities (e.g., God). Again this will depend on the extent of activation of the system, and even in adulthood a frightening situation or immediate shock may prompt a wish for physical contact with a loved one.

Availability (Chapter 1): When the attachment system is activated, an individual is disposed to seek the accessibility and responsiveness of their attachment figure or attachment figures as a safe haven. When the attachment system is not activated, the individual will monitor potential threats, including the threat of inaccessibility or unresponsiveness, which would prompt the system's activation. The form and extent of accessibility and responsiveness that are sought will depend on circumstances. This is part of what makes the concept of 'availability' potentially confusing. In *Separation* (1973, p. 234), Bowlby asserted that "only when an attachment figure is both accessible and potentially responsive can he, or she, be said to be truly available." This means that physical accessibility of the caregiver is not enough; the perception of a caregiver as available as a safe haven depends also on the caregiver's attentional responsiveness. From later childhood onwards, communication may be used to provide indications of an attachment figure's accessibility and responsiveness. However, under conditions of more severe threat and intense activation of the attachment system, physical proximity may still be sought. The individual's sense of the availability of their attachment figure or attachment figures as a safe haven has been termed 'felt security' by Sroufe and Waters.

Conditional strategy (Chapter 3): The term was drawn by Main from evolutionary biology. There it meant that animals sometimes develop alternative strategies to meet the goal of survival or reproduction in response to challenges in the environment. Main applied the term to describe avoidant and resistant attachment behaviour. She felt that avoidant and resistant behaviour reflect alterations in the attention given by an individual to their attachment figures. Avoidant attachment represents a minimisation of attention to attachment figures and, as a result, a minimisation of attachment behaviour. Resistant attachment represents a maximisation of attention to concerns about the availability of the attachment figure and feelings of frustration. Both conditional strategies tend to be less effective in soothing the child than a secure attachment strategy, but in (caregiving) environments with unavailable or inconsistently available attachment figures, these strategies may have advantages.

Disorganisation (Chapter 4): Observable behaviour in the infant or preschool Strange Situation that indicates conflict (expression of different behavioural patterns towards the caregiver, e.g., approach and avoidance), confusion and/or apprehension towards the attachment figure when the child is distressed (and the attachment system is activated). These behaviours might, in different ways, suggest disruption of the attachment behavioural system, perhaps brought about by a state of 'fright without solution' caused by alarming or inexplicable caregiver behaviour in response to child distress. Conflicted, confused, and/or apprehensive behaviour shown towards the caregiver does not necessarily imply that the child has been maltreated. Alternative explanations for these behaviours may be that the caregiver sometimes showed frightening or frightened behaviour towards the child as a result of previous trauma or current psychological distress (e.g., as a result of multiple socio-economic adversities). Repeated or major separations from the parent may also cause disorganised behaviours in children.

Safe haven (Chapter 1): Someone who (or something that) provides comfort and protection in times of potential alarm or distress (i.e., when the attachment system is activated). The attachment system prompts individuals to turn to an attachment figure or attachment figures as a safe haven when alarmed, though this may or not be reflected in the individual's observable behaviour (Chapter 3).

Secure base (Chapter 1): Someone who supports exploration when the attachment system is not activated, that is, the child can explore the environment when s/he is confident that their attachment figure is available to provide support when needed.

Sensitivity (Chapter 3): As defined by Ainsworth, the ability of a caregiver to i) perceive and to ii) interpret accurately the signals and communications implicit in an infant's behaviour and, given this understanding, to iii) respond to them appropriately and iv) promptly. Ainsworth developed a scale for assessing caregiver sensitivity. Various other measures of sensitivity have subsequently been developed by attachment researchers. Not all of them measure sensitivity as technically defined by Ainsworth.

State of mind with respect to attachment (Chapter 5): This is the standard term for 'what the Adult Attachment Interview measures'. State of mind with respect to attachment refers to the manner in which a person is able to attend to and communicate about attachment-related experiences. Main et al.'s study of responses to the Adult Attachment Interview prompts showed that there are patterns in the manner of answering, ranging from directing attention away from these attachment-related events and feelings (e.g., by idealising the situation and limit recall to concrete memories) to directing attention towards attachment-related events and feelings (e.g., by vividly recollecting their past and present relationships to a point where they lose track of the question). In the Adult Attachment Interview, four classifications of state of mind with respect to attachment are given to these speech patterns; see Attachment Classifications. Parents' state of mind with respect to attachment has been consistently (moderately) linked to the quality of their children's attachment relationship with them.

Unresolved attachment state of mind (Chapter 5): An unresolved attachment state of mind occurs when an adult has experienced a significant loss or traumatic abuse experience (usually of/by an attachment figure) and has not processed this event well. When the event is discussed, the discourse becomes confused, contradictory, or displays lapses in reasoning about the event (e.g., self-blame; confusion as to whether someone is alive or dead); the adult cannot think about the event or monitor his or her discourse about it in a structured and concise manner.

INDEX

Note: Page numbers in *italics* indicate a figure and page numbers in **bold** indicate a table on the corresponding page.

Printed in the United States
by Baker & Taylor Publisher Services